THE SALES STRATEGIST

6 Breakthrough Sales Strategies To Win New Business

WARREN KURZROCK

D1292635

IRWIN
Professional Publishing®
Chicago • London • Singapore

This publication is designed to provide accurate and authoritative information in regard to the subject matter covered. It is sold with the understanding that neither the author or the publisher is engaged in rendering legal, accounting, or other professional service. If legal advice or other expert assistance is required, the services of a competent professional person should be sought.

From a Declaration of Principles jointly adopted by a Committee of the American Bar Association and a Committee of Publishers.

Times Mirror
Higher Education Group

Library of Congress Cataloging-in-Publication Data

Kurzrock, Warren.
    The sales strategist : 6 breakthrough sales strategies to win new
business / Warren Kurzrock.
        p.   cm.
    Includes index.
    ISBN 0-7863-0738-2
    1. Sales management.   I. Title.
HF5438.4.K87   1996
658. 8'1—dc20   96–33883

Printed in the United States of America
1 2 3 4 5 6 7 8 9 0 QBP 3 2 1 0 9 8 7 6

THE SALES STRATEGIST

6 Breakthrough Sales Strategies To Win New Business

Dedication

To Sandy, my wife, partner, supporter, and the mother of three great salespeople—Sue, Beth, Mike.

P R E F A C E

As painful as it may seem to many salespeople who work in the corporate sales trenches, selling techniques have not changed much over the years. There have been additions to their toolboxes, of course. These enhancements include laptop computers, slick visuals, sales tools, databases, value-added services, and hard-earned knowledge about products, applications, and customers. However, the art of selling has largely remained at status quo; it didn't need to change since it always did the job . . . until now!

Case in point: a 16th-century religious group, in instructing its "field men" in the art of making converts, used this pattern:

1. Make contact

2. Gain confidence

3. Establish conviction

4. Gain conversion

5. Work for continuance

Certainly selling skills or processes have moved beyond this ancient series of steps. Any professional salesperson knows how to plan a sales call, probe for customer needs, and handle sales resistance. Selling has become more customer focused, more interactive, and new techniques *do* surface. One-to-one selling will always be challenging (and frustrating) simply because every customer is different and unique in his or her personality, values, needs, wants, style, and reactions. Even though the five-step formula used 500 years ago resembles the approach of today, selling is still an art, a set of skills that needs to be employed differently with each customer, and sometimes differently with the same customer (from call to call).

However, the business-to-business selling game has changed. The one-to-one selling skills and techniques will continue to improve incrementally (and slowly!) and there are no magic formulas or breakthroughs in sight. Nonetheless, something is needed to deal with corporate changes.

For example, the sales interface has dramatically and swiftly changed. Important decisions are no longer made by one person in most corporations, and usually there are multiple decision makers involved. Worse yet, decision makers may retreat to a committee to diffuse the risk of a bad decision or to try to reach a consensus. One-to-one selling skills are still important, *but* a new set of tools and skills are needed to funnel each decision maker's needs or convictions into a consensus pattern.

Another change or problem related to the increased numbers of players involved in each decision is access. Involving more people affects available selling time and gaining access when you need it. While seeing more people within an account (and selling each one!) is time consuming and challenging, the frustration is increased by the access inhibitors: travel, voice mail, meetings, and heavier workloads.

The third major change is the excessive demands made by accounts who are working through their own problems. Most companies in today's economy are suffering from meager profits—or losses—and have undergone corporate surgery (downsizing, reengineering). As a result, they demand more quality, faster response time, more service, lower prices, stronger relationships, and so on. Simultaneously, the competition is tougher than ever before because your competitors need the business, too. There are also fewer (but larger) accounts for which to compete.

The conclusion should be obvious: Selling skills are important and always will be in gaining decisions. However, with today's business-to-business selling problems—more decision makers and group decisions, difficulties in gaining access to the right people, and heavier demands and competition—selling must reach another level. Let's call it the strategic level.

This is not to imply that "strategic" selling is a magic formula, or visibly different from traditional selling skills. Strategies could not exist without the selling tactics that make them work. Strategy makes selling skills work better and utilizes them more efficiently with heightened focus and professionalism. In other words, selling skills may be likened to software, and the strategy to an operating system.

While selling skills are arguably an art, strategy is more of a science. It is less reactive and tactical, more structured, and, in the final analysis, is driven by your ability to think, analyze, and plan. However, selling and strategizing are like Siamese twins—totally attached. In today's market, one cannot operate effectively without the other. This book will help salespeople reach a higher level, while finding better ways to hone and utilize their professional selling skills.

ACKNOWLEDGMENTS

The Sales Strategist is dedicated to the many thousands of professional salespeople, sales trainers, and sales managers that Porter Henry & Co. staffers have trained or worked with during the 50 years of our existence. We have learned as much from our clients as they have learned from us.

I would also like to acknowledge the ideas and input from sales executives and their organizations that partnered with us in 1995 to develop our Strategic Business Development course. They provided research opportunities, recommendations, validation, and access to their sales forces. This knowledge and experience helped define some of the key strategies discussed in this book.

In a word—thanks!

Barbara Yoli and Paul Nichols,
Arrow Electronics

Ted Twinny,
SmithKline Beecham

Mark Vitello,
Fisons Pharmaceuticals

Vince Agnew and Dave Fink,
Sony Consumer Products

Jeffrey Grinnell,
Lever Brothers Company

Don Sterkel,
Time Distribution Services

Isabel Kerson,
L'Oreal Cosmetic and Fragrance, Inc.

Keith Vassau and Henk van Lunenburg,
the Upjohn Company

Mark Van Schuyver and Doug Willner,
M&M Mars

Finally, I owe a debt of gratitude to the Porter Henry management team: Bill Voelkel, Paula Murray, and Richard Holmes. Since 1988, they have shared the vision that a strategic architecture was needed for the 1990s in order to enhance selling skills in the quest for new business. They, along with our staff, have contributed significant ideas and experience in the development and validation of the strategies described in this book.

TABLE OF CONTENTS

THE SALES STRATEGIST

6 Breakthrough Sales Strategies To Win New Business

How to Survive in Tomorrow's Marketplace

THE CHALLENGE OF THE 90s:
STRATEGIC BUSINESS DEVELOPMENT

This book is about sales strategies, *not* selling skills or tactics. It is a mandate for salespeople to shift gears from selling to strategizing, to move from piecemeal sales calls and tactics to long-term strategies. Is there a difference? You bet! If the difference isn't apparent, you'll quickly learn how sales tactics and strategies complement each other, and often overlap, but are clearly at opposite ends of the sales spectrum. Selling skills are an essential commodity for every professional salesperson, but those salespeople (and sales forces) that depend on selling skills alone will become dinosaurs by the year 2000. If this sounds harsh or foreboding, step back and look at the forces, trends, and events that have wrought dramatic changes in every marketplace and in most accounts.

The last 5 to 10 years have meant fast-paced and unforgiving change for sales managers, salespeople, and marketing executives. Regardless of whether you are "a street fighter" living with your accounts and their problems, a first-line sales manager, or an "ivory tower" executive looking at sales figures that may depress you, you must be experiencing the change. The classic symptoms are lower-than-expected sales figures and anemic profits, but you have to look further to find the causes, the problems, and the solutions. It's easy to blame the recession since no one can pinpoint when it started (late 1980s), or if and when it went away (mid-1990s), but it certainly had an impact. You can also point to health care reform, the high-tech revolution, merger-mania, the Gulf War, and other domestic and worldwide events. These events together have created change in most companies. As a result, trends have surfaced in every industry, from industrial products to consumer packaged goods, from health care to financial services. These trends have created obstacles that can be hurdled only by salespeople with a long-term and strategic account perspective. In other words, salespeople and sales forces need to arm themselves with *both* selling skills and effective sales strategies. Let's look at the impact these forces have had on the account selling scene. Do these trends, challenges, and scenarios look familiar?

THE 90s LANDSCAPE

Below is a sampling of major changes and obstacles that selling tactics alone will not solve. Most of these challenges require a strategic solution.

■ Above all, customers are smarter than ever. Their technology has caught up with or exceeded yours. Decision makers can access data instantly and can communicate more effectively and faster. They have the answers before salespeople can ask the questions. High-tech tools such as optical scanners, networking, and the Internet have created instant databases and communication vehicles.

■ Decision making has become diffused; it's often difficult to identify who the decision maker is or even how to access him or her. Influencers are harder to reveal or pinpoint, and many decisions once handled by individuals are now shunted off to nebulous committees or advisory teams. When was the last time you lost a sale because the competition located the real decision maker or found the key to the corporate maze first? Access to peripatetic top-level executives is usually required to sell high-ticket contracts or to build alliances.

■ Unless your company is different, the new product offerings have multiplied geometrically, creating a sense of overload and challenging salespeople to move what's hot or what's most profitable. Without strategies for major account penetration and acquisition, many salespeople will take the path of least resistance—to sell what they can. Good strategy use, on the other hand, forces in-depth analysis of each account and identifies the high-potential opportunities, while moving the products or services that are best for the account and for you.

■ There's a huge dichotomy among buyers—some want quality (today's buzzword) and the rest want value (a euphemism for low price). A big problem for the sales professional is reading between the lines to find out what each one really wants. An even bigger problem is having to deal with decision makers in the same organization with dual or conflicting needs or priorities (quality versus value). Sandwiched between quality and value is the demand for value-added services. Value-added means "free services." It is a marketing tool requiring both discretion and allocation as to who gets value and how much to give.

■ In many instances, sales cycles are getting stretched out, a trend that gives decision makers more time to stall, negotiate, make demands, and find alternate suppliers. It certainly challenges the salesperson's ability to stay in tune, follow the track, and deal with a plethora of frustrating obstacles. A strategy helps maintain the focus and direction over time and encourages the sales rep to deal with random events. It enables the salesperson to communicate all along the loop, and it prepares him or her for the long and frustrating path to success.

■ There's also a strong movement toward partnership selling and long-term alliances. Everyone, including both sellers and buyers, talks about partnering in their conversations and literature, but very little happens by design. Most partnerships arise out of need and exist between individuals based on personal relationships. Unfortunately, when one individual moves on, the partnership is instantly dissolved, and the salesperson then has to start over. In a perfect world, the right people can build a partnership between companies or at least between company teams. This requires strategizing.

■ Paramount among the challenges facing salespeople today are the nemesis twins, downsizing and reengineering. Together they have changed the corporate horizon permanently. By turning processes and people upside down, most companies have suddenly altered the pecking order, changed the contacts and relationships, and introduced new expectations for conducting their businesses. The changes in each account are substantial yet different from every other account. As a result, salespeople are being challenged to be more creative, to find new techniques, new tools, new relationships, and new routes for winning the business.

In the face of these dramatic challenges, the sales force and its eclectic support teams (upper management, line sales managers, technical experts, staff support, and more) need to change. The challenge is to shift gears from one-stop, transactional selling (driven by tactics) to long-term strategies designed to build alliances and long-term relationships.

SELLING TACTICS VERSUS SALES STRATEGIES

What's the difference between selling tactics and strategic know-how? Like night and day, they overlap but are quite different. Here's a simple metaphor. To play tennis, you need specific skills or tactics such as hitting overheads, having a good forehand or backhand, and so on. However, once the skills are mastered, the serious tennis players focus on a strategy or set of strategies for each match: playing to an opponent's weakness (such as a poor backhand), rushing the net for easy put-away shots, avoiding risky shots, and so on. In selling, the same skill/tactic versus strategy differences exist. For example, handling an objection is a tactic, but planning a series of calls over time to identify needs and problems that you or your company can solve is a strategy. Tactical skills are needed to implement the strategy, hence an overlap. Let's draw some clear-cut distinctions. A tactic is exercised instantly; you simply do it. On the other hand, a strategy is long term. While you should plan a call, it's done in seconds or minutes. A strategy that takes weeks, months, or even years to implement requires a more comprehensive plan.

A tactic is something you execute by yourself. A strategy often requires support from other members of the team such as technicians, higher-level managers, and so on. As indicated earlier, a tactic is a single act using your talent, but a strategy requires many "acts" or events including tactics but also utilizes meetings, research, planning, and sales calls. A strategy is a scheme or plan for a long-term series of connected sales calls and related activities designed to give you an advantage in achieving specific sales goals with an account. See Exhibit 1.1 for a picture of how tactics and strategies differ.

An important point to remember about strategies is that there is no limit to the number or type you can use. Something as simple as seeking a small sample or trial order on a series of calls can be considered as a doable strategy. Strategies don't have to be complex, but they do require creativity and planning. Like any long-term mission or campaign, a plan

E X H I B I T   1.1

Sales Tactic	vs.	Sales Strategy
■ Instinctive, reflex action		■ Cognitive; requires creative thinking
■ Fits with other sales skills/tactics		■ Part of an overall process
■ Done quickly		■ Long term: takes significant time
■ Part of sales call plan		■ Focus of long-range plan
■ Single skill or action		■ Requires many actions, including sales calls, research, planning
■ Done individually		■ Often requires support of a "team"
■ Used on every sales call		■ For high-potential accounts only
■ Required to achieve sales call objective		■ Required for long-term penetration and goal achievement
■ Needed to sell		■ Needed to position salesperson, gain access, differentiate offer, use skills

is required to keep on track and to communicate responsibilities if others are involved. Most important, in a typical strategic sale a number of defined strategies may be combined to generate results.

The rapid changes in today's marketplace are creating dinosaurs of products, companies, and salespeople who can't change. As a salesperson or sales manager, you too must change and take a more strategic approach to offset and overcome the blockades created by the dynamic forces in the marketplace. How? Build your strategic abilities and don't depend on selling skills alone. Start by looking at high-potential accounts in depth, and with future focus, rather than by making piecemeal sales calls alone. Concentrate on a handful of high-potential accounts at a time, and analyze the players, the culture, the competition, how your product fits with their needs, and so on. The opportunities will eventually surface. Then zero in on a few key accounts with the greatest potential and design a long-range strategic penetration plan including realistic goals, strategies for achieving them (be creative), and realistic timetables. Most important, build a passion for executing your strategy, mobilizing help as needed to achieve your goal. Becoming strategic in your thought process is a challenge, but no one ever said selling was easy! This book will provide the specifics on proven strategies and how to execute them, but the creativity and passion must be provided by the seller.

SALES STRATEGY REINVENTED

In the chapters that follow, we'll explore six interacting (and/or independent) strategies that have been reinvented by Porter Henry & Company, working with the sales forces of hundreds of Fortune 500 clients. Why reinvented? While we've been in business since 1945, we don't claim to have invented sales training or every form of sales strategy. However, as active participants in the changes and trends affecting sales force productivity (our only business), we have, through consulting, training, fieldwork, and significant research, defined and developed a number of high-impact sales strategies.

This book will deal with six formidable strategies that we've identified, defined, added value to, and provided a structure for. Our clients have validated each through experience and application. The six strategies listed below are covered in separate chapters that follow:

- Team selling
- Consultative selling
- Selling value-added services
- Sales negotiating
- Access strategy
- Alignment strategy

Each strategy has a "name" as part of the definition process. The names serve only to identify each one; the value is in understanding the strategy and being able to execute it. The strategies can be used separately or in combination. (See Chapter 8,. "Putting It All Together"). In application, they may overlap to work together or to have a synergistic impact on a specific account. However, there are common elements for each to provide a solid framework for both implementation and training, including a "model" or series of steps, specific requirements for planning and skill use in execution, and tips on how to implement over time. If any of these strategies can be implemented on *one sales call,* it simply isn't a strategy.

Another fact to recognize is that there is an unlimited number of strategies or hybrids available. If someone were compiling a portfolio of sales strategies, they might include concepts like: using entertainment effectively, setting up a "coach" within an account, using a wedge to gain a foothold (a sample product or trial period), focusing on a market niche, creating more visibility by accelerating the contact frequency, and so on.

However, the six strategies we have selected are the most powerful we know. They have evolved quickly to a state-of-the-art level in recent years, and above all, they work!

A word of caution. Do not confuse these strategies with short-term tactics or skills such as "reading" personality styles, using third-party references, or making a group presentation. These items are tactics or skills, not long-term strategies. Of course, some of them may be important in implementing a strategy and, therefore, will be part of it.

Another distinction that needs to be made is how to position sales strategies as they relate to corporate sales strategy. There are differences and similarities. Corporate sales strategies are broader and apply to most accounts. They are usually global in that they cover a broad area and are often general. For example, one industrial company's strategy is to be the low-priced vendor; a high-tech manufacturer's strategy is to dominate its markets by having multiple channels of distribution; a chemical company differentiates itself (strategy) by providing its distributors with intensive training; a service organization has structured a partnership program that it markets strategically to major accounts that meet certain criteria.

There is certainly no conflict between the corporate strategies and the sales strategies that will be covered here. In fact, you'll quickly see how they support each other. The major difference between the sales strategies we'll discuss and the strategies emanating from corporate headquarters is that any of the sales strategies can be *initiated by salespeople* based on their firsthand perception of opportunities within each account. Most of the strategies that we'll discuss serve as springboards for corporate strategies.

In addition to selling benefits to satisfy current needs, you will be armed with strategies that can be used long term to capitalize on opportunities. The end result is improved account penetration, shortened sales cycles, solid account relationships, and greater customer satisfaction.

To further delineate the difference between strategies and tactics (or skills) let's take a real-life example. You will be able to identify certain skills as they are utilized in executing the strategy.

A REAL-LIFE CASE STUDY

Terry Adams, a key account manager for TastyBrand, a major consumer packaged goods manufacturer, has been calling on the headquarters of General Grocery for many years with great success. His six product lines have grown significantly within the account, and he has built good relationships with the various people he deals with such as the merchandising manager, two different category managers (buyers), the advertising and promotions director, and a number of others. One of his frustrations has been his inability to get his relatively new Oat Bran cereal into the General Grocery chain. While he has promoted it frequently on sales calls and received some positive feedback, the bottom line is that he has been told, "We just don't have space for another cereal item; after all, we have three of your cereals on our shelves now" Terry, of course, has used his data to show that his new product has a greater market share than some of his competitors' brands, but to no avail.

Terry met with his boss, Todd Atkins, a regional vice president for TastyBrand, and decided it was critical to get Oat Bran cereal approved for distribution at General Grocery. They began to formulate a strategy, which admittedly would take a lot of time and effort. If successful, the rewards would certainly be an adequate payback.

After a significant amount of discussion, they decided that Harry Newton, vice president of category management at General Grocery, was the real problem and probably the key decision maker or ratifier. Harry is a little pompous and slightly dictatorial; he's tough to overcome when he has his mind made up. To add to the problem, Harry is difficult to access. Terry and Todd both agreed that they had to involve other decision makers in the process who could use their influence or authority to motivate Harry. They agreed on a plan that would probably take six months, and it would reach a climax at the next business review with General Grocery. It involved a number of actions by the TastyBrand team that had to be carefully orchestrated over the next few months. In brief, these were the steps they thoroughly plotted out and implemented to form an integrated strategy.

1. Todd Atkins agreed to have TastyBrand's Space Management Department do an in-store space study within a sample of General Grocery stores. The department used its computer program to do a "what if" space management test comparing competitors' product sales versus TastyBrand's Oat Bran cereal, using market share data and space allocation. While there was only a 1 percent difference in market share, based on the number of facings allocated and the number of stores in the chain, this translated into a gross profit increase of $22,000 a year for General Grocery. While not significant in the big picture, it was certainly more dramatic than the "1 percent difference" the category manager had rejected as "trivial" on previous sales calls.

2. Because both Terry and Todd, in their earlier discussions, anticipated this same reaction from Harry, part of their plan involved some behind-the-scenes selling to both Harry and others in the General Grocery executive group. They recognized that subtle pressure from others was necessary to convert Harry. As a result, they agreed to contact one of Harry's peers with an interest in getting this new brand introduced, as well as Harry's boss. The plan was that Todd (because of his rank) would handle the higher-level (top-to-top) call with General's executive vice president, and Terry would make calls on Harry Newton and his staff. They agreed to select other objectives for the calls, but to bring up the new brand and include significant benefits (the health trend, heavy promotional activity, and the significant profit advantage over the competition).

3. The next step was to occur at the General Grocery business review. Terry and Todd planned to review TastyBrand's entire product line in terms of potential movement, distribution, and profits. They also planned to do a major competitive analysis featuring the new Oat Bran cereal and its advantages; the region analyst would accompany them to help with the presentation and to justify the study's results. Most important, they anticipated a healthy discussion afterward (triggered by planned, leading questions) to get the previous players to endorse this concept and, in the process, influence Harry to make a favorable decision. While Harry did not agree to immediate distribution at the business review, he *did* admit the product now had some merit for consideration.

4. Follow-up calls on all the "players" were planned, but only one with Harry was necessary. A week after the business review, he agreed to pilot the new product at 10 of the chain's flagship stores. Obviously, the sales strategy had worked.

What was the strategy? Actually, a number of strategies were planned and utilized by the players to keep the mission on track and make it happen. For example, they used a *consultative approach* to gather data and illuminate a costly problem. *Team selling* was integrated throughout, from the initial planning session, through all the necessary steps to achieve their goal. An *access strategy* was used to evaluate the various influences and then to get them in order to have an impact on the ultimate decision maker.

The point of this case history is that (1) real-life strategies are often integrated into a comprehensive plan of attack, and (2) the ultimate goal and the situation must dictate which menu of strategies should work best. However, in learning strategies or for training salespeople in how to create, evolve, and use strategies, it's desirable to address each strategy separately. This provides an opportunity to practice the strategy and try it on for size. Strategies, because of their creative and conceptual nature, are best learned one at a time. As a result, we will "practice what we preach" by allocating a separate chapter to each strategy. Chapter 8 will provide the tools for combining them.

BENEFITS OF STRATEGIC SELLING

The obvious benefit for taking a strategic approach to selling is to make sales. No one can deny that this is the ultimate return on investment for training, time, and resources used in executing the strategy. However, there are other significant side benefits that should be emphasized, also. If no extra sales were ever attributed specifically to a strategy per se, significant benefits would nevertheless accrue.

Consider the "two heads are better than one" benefit. Strategies often call for involvement of other people—bosses, staff, and specialists. This "brainstorming" effort is creative and will often generate the key idea or concept that can tilt the sale or penetrate the account.

Team building is another plus. While many outsiders consider the salesperson the typical "Lone Ranger" of the territory, being a loner is ancient history. Bringing others into the planning and implementation process is not only supportive, but also causes all the players to be more motivated and focused.

Strategizing is a cognitive process, and like most creative endeavors, it is very challenging. The process trains people to think clearer, to overcome obstacles, and to devise new and better approaches. In the process, salespeople also develop themselves.

Another major benefit is that strategies differentiate you from your competition. A series of well-planned and thoughtfully implemented strategies reinforces corporate goals and emphasizes your capabilities, mission, and desire to satisfy customer needs. The strategic process itself differentiates you in the eyes of your customers.

Most important, strategies utilize your resources in the most productive way. Implementation capitalizes on value-added services such as customer service, field experts, upper-echelon managers, and all the resources your company provides such as sales aids, computers, data, delivery and service, and so on.

YOUR STRATEGIC ROAD MAP

As indicated, a strategy is long-term and consists of many tactics (steps, actions) folded into a comprehensive action plan. However, it's also important to recognize that there are basically two types of tactics, those involving face-to-face selling, and those requiring planning and thinking skills. In the strategies that follow, you'll first be introduced to a model of each (the big picture, or overview) followed by a description of the specific tactics used in implementing the strategy. To distinguish the two types of tactics we've provided these icons or visual signs:

☐ Indicates tactics that require *non-selling* actions: planning, research, internal meetings, analysis.

◇ Indicates tactics that call for selling actions, face-to-face activities with customers such as probing, negotiating, presenting benefits, networking, and so on.

While the differences between the two types of tactics are not great, you'll find that the challenge of developing a strategic approach to account penetration places more emphasis on the non-selling tactics.

As you read the pages that follow, you'll see that the six strategies we have delineated have models and tactics (steps). The rationale is that strategies, being of a conceptual nature, need as much structure as possible so they can be readily learned. The other important idea to carry with you as you read these pages is that no strategy will ever be complete. We've evolved these strategies over many years with the help of thousands of salespeople and sales managers. I suspect that, as you read about each one, some things will be familiar and others will be new and different. These are proven and solid strategies, and they work. But each can be adapted and improved in use, and your reading will trigger many ideas on how you can implement the strategies with your own accounts. That's what strategizing is all about: creative, thoughtful, flexible plans that generate significant future sales results.

2

CHAPTER

Team Selling Strategy

WHAT TEAM SELLING IS AND IS NOT

Team selling strategy is a powerful tool when used properly. Unfortunately, there are many salespeople and sales managers who think of team selling as "making a joint call" with another salesperson, a sales manager, a specialist, or someone from upper management. Not so! While a joint call might be *one tactic* in the strategy, team selling, as a strategy, has a life of its own.

Like other strategies, it is a series of actions or events over time and often requires more than one support person. The ultimate goal of team selling is to penetrate accounts and sell through gaining access to account decision makers by optimizing your resources (the "team"). As a result, it requires careful orchestration and management, not only because the team must function as one unit, but also because team selling resources (people) need to be allocated where you can get the best return on investment. As you'll quickly see, team selling is a major process to add to your strategy toolbox. However, you should also recognize what team selling is not. It's certainly *not:*

- A single sales call with a support person to help you close a piece of business.

- A number of support people recruited at the last minute for a major group presentation. As one frustrated client put it: "Our salespeople and specialists often do their planning for a major presentation on the elevator—hopefully the account is on a high floor!"
- Bringing in the top guns for the "big" presentation. While senior executives from headquarters are often effective in building credibility, team selling requires many steps to prepare the team, to establish relationships, and to sell products and services.

The team selling strategy is powerful, proven, and will work big time in the right situation. However, it must be implemented in a thorough and thoughtful manner. This chapter will provide the nuts and bolts of how the pros execute it.

WHY TEAMWORK IN SALES?

Corporate America is in love with teams, so it should come as no surprise that the concept of teamwork, which started as a fad, has now become a major sales strategy. Consider the hot trends that started in the late 1980s and burgeoned into the 1990s and it's easy to see why teamwork per se has become the latest fad. When you consider the buzzwords of the times—quality, diversity, empowerment, reengineering—it becomes apparent that the link between these management concepts is the *team.*

The quality movement functions around quality teams (circles) who meet frequently to improve workplace productivity. While diversity does not depend on teamwork, it maintains that teams work better when you have participants with diverse backgrounds. Empowerment, which started as empowering *individuals,* has moved quietly and safely to "empowered teams." Reengineering quite often uses teams to redefine processes. If teamwork works effectively (arguably!) in these other endeavors or missions, why not in sales? This movement has created a case strong enough to initiate team selling in many organizations, hence the birth of a new sales strategy—team selling. The real reason for the success of team selling, however, lies in the fact it was desperately needed to *meet customer needs* and to *unlock decision-making processes.*

Team selling strategy works well for many organizations. Like the other species of teams in quality, reengineering, and traditional problem solving and decision making, there are some downsides. Most occur through misuse. Many innovative organizations have used team selling to penetrate accounts, improve sales productivity, and alter the myth that a salesperson has to operate as a "Lone Ranger." Others have set up virtual teams, which have all the facade of great teamwork, but provide little more than a cosmetic platform for advertising or as a shallow promise to clients and potential buyers.

Team selling, if pursued properly, provides many benefits to both vendor sales teams and customers in terms of increased performance and customer satisfaction. Before you consider this strategy and how to execute it effectively, let's look at some problems.

▗━ R E D   F L A G

BEWARE OF TEAM SELLING POTHOLES

Recognize that team selling is simple in concept, almost an extension of what salespeople do on a regular basis. Having said that, I must caution that there are certain finite differences that require changes in both process, selling skills, and execution. The differences, while small, are critical to ensure that team selling, as a strategy, works well for you.

The best way to illuminate the problems in using this powerful tool is to document, in brief, some real-life, team selling scenarios that did *not* work. The good news is that these situations were corrected and ultimately turned into strategic tools that exceeded expectations.

- A major insurance company, marketing through brokers, adopted a team selling approach and devised a comprehensive strategy that focused each team on a handful of accounts. The team process started with intensive team meetings to analyze each account in depth. Next, each team developed a detailed marketing plan to help a specific broker organization "pull through" more of its insurance business. However, when it came time to make individual sales calls or team sales calls no one but the *salesperson* on each team (other team members were adjusters, marketing staff, underwriters, etc.) was available; the other team members conveniently found excuses for *not* making sales calls. After researching a mix of teams, we found a key problem: *there was no one in charge.* A basic rule for any successful teamwork is that there must be a "captain"; someone must be accountable and provide leadership. While this role can be rotated, it needs to be clearly identified and defined. A second problem was procedural: finding a method to free up and prioritize the time of supporting team members, all of whom had other jobs.

- A manufacturer of pet food and supplies set up team forays to make group presentations and sales calls on veterinarians and pet food outlets. Each team consisted of detail salespeople, a technical specialist, and distributor salespeople (who actually wrote the order). One problem surfaced that initially handicapped the project— geography. Most team members lacked proximity to one another (and to various accounts) so added travel and extensive phone and e-mail communication was needed. These problems spurred the company to make adjustments before continuing the team selling strategy. The changes involved a communication procedure that was effective, saved time, and eliminated extensive travel. Equally important, the roles of each team member were specifically defined.

These may seem like simple mistakes, but they were made by organizations that took great pains to structure the team selling format, including training in team building and team selling, and recognized the need to build trust among the team members. While it's relatively easy to create teams and institute team selling, there are potholes and obstacles, not the least of which is getting an individual to surrender his or her identity and become a dedicated team contributor. Team chemistry is always critical.

VARIATIONS OF TEAM SELLING

While team selling may sound like it defines itself, nothing is further from the truth. One dilemma a team player needs to deal with is determining what type of team selling he or she is going to use. The decision may not be yours alone since some types of team selling are mandated by corporate headquarters while others are initiated by the salesperson. In brief, there are basically three formats for executing the team selling strategy: dedicated teams, cross-functional teams, and ad hoc teams.

Dedicated teams are mandated by headquarters and you'll certainly know if that's the way you should operate. A dedicated team usually consists of salespeople and support staff with total responsibility for a geographic area, a set of accounts, or even one major account. The team is totally committed in terms of focus, time, and effort to pursuing business in its dedicated area of responsibility. The team remains together and its permanent mission is to manage and penetrate the team's assigned account(s). How they organize, and determine calls or responsibilities, is often determined by the team. This type of team selling generally works best for large sales forces with critical mass marketplaces (customers and channels of distribution in close proximity) and is often germane to products/services that are high-tech, involve capital equipment, substantial repeat business, or long sales cycles.

A second type of sales team is called a *cross-functional team*. This strategy often involves team selling at various levels in the account organization. A classic example is the consumer packaged goods manufacturer who might sell directly to major food and drug chains. At the retail level, it frequently has a sales force calling on retail store managers and local headquarters, writing orders, merchandising, selling promotions, identifying store problems, and so on. At the chain headquarters, however, the key account managers have the responsibility to get distribution approval on new products, sell promotions to the category manager, handle credit problems, and so on. Most important, there has to be coordination between these cross-functional teams so the left hand knows what the right hand is doing. Communication is key, and it's complicated because a key account manager may be working with X salespeople on one account and Y salespeople on another. Since there is usually no direct reporting relationships between both functions, and proximity is often lacking, coordination of their joint efforts is essential. To complicate the paradigm, upper management and different teams often "team up" for joint sales calls.

The *ad hoc sales team* is recruited for a specific mission. Typically, the salesperson senses an account situation that requires support, either from his or her boss, technical experts, or others, and rallies the team for a specific "mission." The mission may involve strategizing, individual calls (at different levels or with different people), or team presentation(s). The key limitation for the ad hoc team is that most of the people have other jobs to perform and have to be recruited to support the team selling strategy and motivated to participate on the team until the mission is completed. This should *not* be confused with asking your boss to accompany you for a major presentation or to help make the sale!

Team selling gets complicated beyond the three formats described above. Even the dedicated or cross-functional teams may have to shift gears into an ad hoc format and bring in temporary or dedicated experts, specialists, and high-ranking executives on occasion. Regardless of the format you follow, team selling can be a complex strategy, shifting its "shape" and point of contact to meet the needs of the account.

Regardless of which option you use for implementing the team selling strategy, this chapter will provide a useful framework and models for improving execution. The team selling strategy is very situational, and its use is often dictated by customer needs and actions. How you use the tools and ideas that are provided depends to a large degree on your own perceptions of the account and your creativity as a team player.

In the pages that follow, you'll recognize that team selling is more than simply getting a technical expert or support person to back you up on a call or key presentation. The team members will have various roles and participate in many activities, including research, planning, team meetings, individual sales calls and group presentations, and even telephone contact with account decision makers. Like any effective team, the roles and process must be defined to optimize impact and results. Communication, teamwork, and planning are key.

Let's look at a real-life example of how the team selling strategy can work.

 CASE STUDY

TEAM SELLING

Pete Adams, a salesman for a computer software producer, recognized quickly that he would need help selling a major pharmaceutical manufacturer on a software system for its sales force. The prospect had recently contracted for laptop computers for its 1,000-person sales force and was seeking competitive bids for an integrated software system that provided performance data, product information, and internal communications capability, among other features. After assessing the situation and the competition, Pete estimated he had a 60 to 75 percent probability of getting a $500,000 start-up order.

After a few initial calls to scope the project and start building relationships, he recruited a team consisting of himself; Tony Marconi, a technical design specialist; Joan Gibbons, his division manager; and Larry Emerson, vice president of customer service. Since some team members were based in different cities, they held a teleconference to determine roles, assignments, and an overall strategy.

From this meeting emerged a strategy for individual calls on key people at the pharmaceutical manufacturer, matching callers at various levels with comparable titles and interests within the prospect company. For example, Harry Emerson planned a top-to-top call to the head of management information services, since service was an issue with her, and the team believed it would sound less threatening as a solo call.

CASE STUDY continued

Some team members contributed design research so they could ultimately make a custom-design recommendation that fit the company's exact needs. Each call was orchestrated carefully to either sell or gather information, and the team periodically touched base over a four-month sales cycle that led to a final presentation. Pete made a number of calls on the vice president of sales and his administrative assistant. He also spent a day in the field, riding "shotgun" with a pharmaceutical sales rep to get a firsthand understanding of her communication and data needs.

Just before the key presentation at which they were to present their proposal, the team members became aware that the pharmaceutical company had a recall on a product, which would mean a loss of $100 million in drug sales and could jeopardize or postpone the installation of software.

Pete Adams, as the salesperson and team captain, made two critical decisions before the final presentation, during which all vendors (two competitive vendors included) would make their pitch. First, he got permission from his boss to bring the entire team in a day early for a planning session at a motel adjacent to the pharmaceutical's headquarters. Second, anticipating a budget problem as a result of the product recall, he asked that a financial representative be present. Both moves paid off.

As a result of planning the key sales presentation, the team members were able to define specific roles for each person at this presentation to maximize skills and teamwork. Equally important, they had the time and input to "read" the six to eight pharmaceutical attendees and anticipate their moves and individual needs. Consequently, they were able to direct questions and segments of the presentations to the most appropriate presenter and build on the group dynamics to gain support for their product.

As anticipated, the budget issue came up when the pharmaceutical comptroller indicated they would have to defer the software and equipment purchases until the end of the fiscal year because of the product recall. However, the financial expert on Pete's selling team presented a deferred plan that would enable the pharmaceutical company to pursue both projects (hardware and software) simultaneously and equip the sales force as originally planned. A week later, Pete was notified that his company had won the software contract.

Obviously, this was a team effort that worked. It worked because the team acted as a cohesive unit on independent and group activities, as required. From beginning to end, the actions were taken in concert over six months from the time of inception. The driving force was the team's flexible strategic plan that provided a track to run on.

AN OVERVIEW OF THE TEAM SELLING STRATEGY

Regardless of which type of team selling format you use (or are locked into due to company strategy) you should be using a proven model to execute the strategy. Like other strategies, there are many steps and often a long sales cycle, so the model provides a framework and direction. The team selling model appears in Exhibit 2.1. The rectangular boxes indicate *planning or research activities* or tactics while the diamond-shaped steps call for *selling tactics.* Remember that these icons will be used throughout the text to distinguish selling ($\diamond$) from non-selling ($\square$) tactics (see page 11).

In the first step or tactic, *identify team sell opportunity,* the salesperson assesses the risks and costs involved and determines whether a team selling strategy is the best strategy to accomplish the goal for the account. The second tactic *initiate team action plan* is your trigger for kicking off the campaign or mission and the first critical action for organizing and managing the team's efforts.

The third tactic is *conduct team strategy briefing.* Depending on the scope of the mission and the type of team selling used, there could be a number of team meetings.

Fourth, *execute preliminary actions and sales calls* is a series of individual or joint calls and other actions involving various team members. It is the start of the team selling process and strategy.

Plan and implement the key sales call is often the high point in team selling, since it usually involves important members of both your team and the account's in a face-to-face presentation. The key sales call, as we define it, is a group presentation with key players from both sides; it takes the form of a formal business review, your response to a request for proposal, a "finalist" presentation, or a presentation initiated by your team.

The final step, *follow-up,* takes place with team members, individually or jointly, making sales calls, telephone calls, or pursuing other follow-up activities.

In all three team selling formats—dedicated, cross-functional, or ad hoc—the same needs exist. The challenge is for the captain (usually a salesperson) to focus, coordinate, and manage a team (whose members or roles will often change) to the successful completion of a sale (mission, campaign). When finished, the team may or may not disband (depending on format), but the next mission will have similar needs for restarting the team engine. In the following sections, the various steps and tools are covered in depth.

EXHIBIT 2.1

Team Selling Model

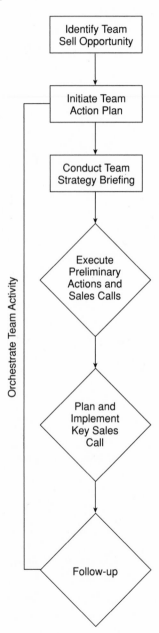

☐ Tactic 1: Identify the Team Sell Opportunity

This tactic may seem like a routine step, but it's critical because it is here that one must determine whether this is *the right opportunity for team support*. While most salespeople will negotiate for all the support they can get on any sales call, team selling commits resources to the cause and the process must be judiciously used and monitored. If not, the only gain will be in selling costs, with little concrete results to back up the decision. There are a number of risks involved in team selling, not the least of which is the cost. As a result, there is a definite need to optimize the strategy, and opportunities need to be carefully weighed and reviewed. When determining which opportunities to commit to, sales managers and salespeople should use the following criteria as guidelines.

■ **Is this a major opportunity?** A substantial end result or opportunity should exist with a high-potential account before you consider team support. This may seem obvious, but it does require that you define what a major opportunity is—$10,000? $100,000? A million-dollar, long-term potential? High probability for success? A new or existing account? Because team selling requires an allocation of resources and risk, the payback, if you succeed, should be significant in terms of short-term or long-term business.

■ **Is team support critical for success?** This is a tough question to ask and a tough one to get a straight answer to. However, it must be asked frequently and should be followed up by other questions that will give you the answers you need to make a hard-nosed (and profitable) decision. If you can accomplish the sales objective by yourself, you should go it alone. Before seeking team selling support, determine if team help will really add a substantial dimension. If it's too early in the sales cycle to really know the potential, for example, then defer the decision on support. Similarly, if you can't persuasively defend your need for support, back off. Reasons you may need team support include special expertise or technical backup, executive help to reach high-level decision makers, assistance in developing a strategy, staff assistance to gather data and do studies, and so on.

■ **Is access to all or many account decision makers essential to making the sale?** If the final decision is being made by one person, or by a few easily accessible decision makers, team selling may not be needed. A frequent by-product of team selling is a face-to-face presentation with members of *both* teams (the "key sales call," as we refer to it in team selling). The key sales call alone will usually surface any hidden decision makers and will certainly bring all of them together so the sales team can help them reach a consensus. Consequently, if you are unable to access one or more of the very influential people in an account, this alone may be a good rationale for endorsing team selling as the strategy to use. Team selling, as you'll see, can surface hidden decision makers in a number of ways.

Team selling works best when there is a major opportunity, when the team is vital to building credibility by adding technical or other support, and when it's critical to bring all the decision makers together—because you need a consensus, or because they can't be accessed individually. In most cases, team selling enables a non-sales member of the team (such as a technical expert) to reach an unavailable decision maker. It also positions a vice president in the selling company to call a vice president in the customer company simply because they are at similar levels in their organizations.

The first step is identifying the team sell opportunity. This forces you to define the opportunity and validate whether it's best to proceed with the opportunity or to use another strategy.

□ Tactic 2: Initiate Team Action Plan

A team action plan is a way of organizing the team so the varied strengths of the team members can be effectively utilized. Equally important, it reinforces the leadership role of the salesperson (as captain of the team) and provides you with a control and planning mechanism to direct the team's activities. A sample action plan appears in Exhibit 2.2.

The team action plan serves as a structure for keeping the team together, forcing good communication, defining roles, developing timetables, and working through the various stages of the team selling process, including follow-up. It's nothing more than a worksheet, and while it can take different formats, putting the action plan in writing is a must. This will reinforce commitment for the team participants and ensure that all critical roles are fulfilled on time, as planned.

An action plan of this type is normally initiated by the salesperson after he or she identifies the need and opportunity for team selling. It will help in recruiting the right people for various stages of the strategy as well. Most important, it will underline the importance of each person's contribution.

Unfortunately, team selling in many organizations often amounts to a support person or a sales manager making a last-minute sales call with a salesperson, either for technical support or to buttress credibility. That's not effective in today's marketplace, and an action plan will eliminate "shooting from the hip."

One of our clients, a large service organization, shared an example of how team selling, without proper structure, can miss the target. The local representative had done her homework with the Cleveland-based account, bringing them to the point where they were considering a million-dollar proposal from different vendors. While she had the inside track, she felt it critical to get key people from her organization involved, particularly for the final presentation. She asked a division manager, based in Toronto, and the vice president of sales to fly in from New York for the formal presentation. However, due to the lack of a team selling strategy (which would have required earlier involvement on the part of the "team") the deal went to a competitor. In the postmortem, one client team member noted: "While we were impressed, all you did was bring in a couple of 'suits' who didn't know our needs or business; we would have preferred hearing more from you, since you had a relationship with some of our key people." Evidently the account manager, who initiated the presentation, got lost in the shuffle.

☐ Tactic 3: Conduct Team Strategy Briefing

The next tactic in the team selling model is to have a team meeting (or several meetings) to brief the team on the account. To play a role, everyone needs to be up to speed on decision makers and influencers, where the gaps are, who has the edge, what the competition has going for it, and what are the account's potential, goals, and objectives. In addition, the team captain (hopefully, the salesperson) should be able to clarify roles and get input from the other people on the team. The team action plan can be modified or enhanced at this point. A major benefit of the team approach is brainstorming or team strategizing. If the team members can contribute to the strategy itself, you'll wind up with a better game plan.

To a certain degree, this is where typical selling skills take over. The individual or joint calls should be delineated based on individual needs, relationships, strengths, or specialties of team members (i.e., "the plant manager at customer X should be called on by our technical specialist so we can make him feel comfortable with our capability"). At this

E X H I B I T   2 . 2

TEAM ACTION PLAN

TEAM ACTION PLAN

1. Identify team members and roles:		Preliminary sales calls	Key sales calls	Other
Team member	**Contribution**			
Bob M. (V.P.)	credibility/presenter		X	
Ed T. (Tech. Mgr.)	expertise	X	X	
Ellen D. (Account Mgr.)	relationship &	X	X	Set up
	presentation skills			key sales
				call

2. Conduct team strategy briefing: Date ___10/9___   Time ___10 am___   Place ___here___

☒ **Plan and implement preliminary calls:**

Team members	Call objective	Target date
Ellen	Arrange logistics of key call	9/15
Ed	Answer two major technical	9/15
	questions with Bill Robbins	
Ellen	Get to know Dave Sims/	9/15
	assess his position	

3. Plan and develop key sales call   Date ___10/17___   Time ___10 am___   Place ___Overlook___

☒ **Plan and implement preliminary calls**   ☒ **Rehearse the presentation**

Team member	Responsibility
Bob M.	Get details of success story with
	Acme Corp.
Ellen	Take charge of handouts
Ed	Produce cost comparison chart

4. Implement follow-up:

Team members	Call objective	Target date
Bob M.	Write letter after call	10/25
Ellen	If we get commitment, she'll	after 10/25
	follow up on delivery. If	
	not, she'll try to close.	

stage planning is key to determine who calls on whom, and what other steps—such as research on a competitive offering, planning the proposal, gaining access to hidden decision makers, and building relationships— are covered. This is normal selling for experienced salespeople, but the danger lies in allowing nonsales team members to make sales calls without some prior coaching (if needed) by the salesperson/captain or other proficient salespeople on the team.

◇ Tactic 4: Execute Preliminary Actions and Sales Calls

Depending on the plan of attack, a variety of actions need to be executed by individuals and possibly by two or more team members in tandem. Based on our experience with hundreds of organizations selling high-ticket items to large, complex accounts, most final decisions in today's marketplace are made by a committee or group. As a result, one goal of team selling is to get the selling team face to face with the client "team." If you can't get in front of the decision makers in full force, there's little chance of winning the game. The long-range goal of team selling (aside from getting the business!) is to set up the key sales call—a group presentation with the key decision makers. Assuming this can be accomplished, it's the best guarantee that *all* the decision makers will surface, and it's the best opportunity to influence a favorable decision. The key sales call will be covered later, but many activities must be accomplished before this event in order to set the stage and eliminate surprises. For example, the following are some actions and calls that need to be taken by various team members in most team selling strategies:

- Research—to find information on the organization, uncover decision makers, and learn more about specific needs.
- Sales calls (or telephone calls)—to unknown or known decision makers, to determine their attitudes, to build relationships, and to do individual selling.
- Team meetings or other communications—to evolve strategy, monitor progress, and determine the next steps.
- Field visits—to installations or branches to meet users and determine needs.

As you can see, there is some homework and much good judgment that goes into this step, so it needs to be carefully orchestrated by the team captain.

RED FLAG

BE PREPARED TO COACH OTHER TEAM MEMBERS

Ideally, a salesperson should be captain of the team, although there are other options for supplying team leadership. One red flag (danger) you need to recognize is that a typical team has a variety of expertise represented among its members. That's the strength of the team, but also the Achilles' heel. The function of the team is to sell; that's what the mission is all about. And while some sales team members may possess good instinctive selling skills naturally developed or from previous selling assignments, others may not. At best, their skills will be rusty or nonexistent.

As a result, the team captain may have to do some peer coaching or even coach a higher-ranking executive. You can't assume that an engineer, a chemist, a programmer, an analyst, or those in other supporting roles can present or sell effectively. This includes directors, vice presidents, or others at levels above your position.

What do you do? You should recruit the people who fit the roles you need for the team; that comes first. Next do a reality check on their selling skills. Depending on the role they may play (participating in presentations, individual sales calls), you should tactfully offer to help and either provide a coaching session or accompany them on calls, for coaching afterward. When doing coaching, (1) reinforce strengths with specific positive comments, (2) focus on one skill at a time (avoid giving them "indigestion"), (3) make suggestions for change tactfully, and (4) provide feedback immediately after the call.

◇ Tactic 5: Plan and Implement the Key Sales Call

The key sales call, with both teams facing off in a group setting, is the most important tactic in effective team selling. It is also the most difficult and challenging, for a variety of reasons, including:

- Group selling requires special skills and is quite different from one-on-one selling.
- The group presentation needs careful orchestration on the part of the presenters, so everyone has a role and can execute at the appropriate moment.

- There is always an unknown element, or potential for surprise. It can come in the form of a difficult objection or question, meeting interruptions, late arrivals or early departures, participation from "unknown" decision makers, and so on.

As a result of the above, it is critical that the team presenters have the know-how (skills) and time to plan the key sales call. While similar to a typical one-on-one sales call, the key sales call or group presentation is different—mainly because of the group dynamics involved.

Research into group dynamics reveals that most groups tend to follow the leader; it's similar to the "herd" concept. Consequently, in any group situation involving three or more people, the group will likely "following the leader" and reach a consensus. This presents two interacting challenges for the selling team:

- Who is the leader and is he/she supportive?
- How can the team get the leader to speak out and influence his or her peers, subordinates, or senior executives?

The answer to both of these challenges lies in planning and executing the key sales call. Most salespeople and sales teams will go to extensive lengths to prepare what they will say and how they will support their presentation with good graphics or visuals, delineating roles for members of the team. However, they will usually fall short in accurately identifying the true leader of the group and getting him or her involved; the latter requires an understanding of group dynamics and a truly interactive meeting.

Here's how it works. The leader who has to be identified has more going for him or her than merely title or authority. While position is important, a number of other characteristics pinpoint the true leader. One method for identifying the leader is our proprietary READ profile. This tool enables you to read the participants and determine where the leadership lies. READ is an acronym representing four characteristics. When applied to account decision makers, the READ profile enables you to compare each one, and predict who the leader will be.

The four dimensions of the READ profile are:

R = Receptivity (to you, your company, and the proposal).

E = Expertise (familiarity with your product/service and application).

A = Authority (rank, title, credibility, power).

D = Dynamics (ability to persuade others).

To use this tool, you simply rank each person high, medium, or low for the four dimensions.

The ideal leader in a customer group would be someone who ranks high in these four characteristics, or certainly in receptivity, authority, and dynamics. This profile will also enable the sales team to pinpoint supporters, experts (on the product/application), and doubters (people who need to be convinced). Supporters are high in receptivity; experts are high in expertise (and hopefully high in receptivity); doubters are low in receptivity. The objective is to identify the leaders, supporters, and receptive experts and encourage them to persuade others through discussion. The more dynamic they are, the better.

Once you understand the concept, the next challenge is planning feedback from the customer team. This is often the shortfall in team selling or group presentations. Most sales teams feel the need to present, present, and present, getting so engrossed in the formal pitch that they leave little room or time for feedback. At best, many presenters leave time for questions at the end, but this does little but raise the obvious ones or leave people looking at their watches. Recently, one paper goods manufacturer hired us to train account managers to move away from formal, lengthy "data dump" presentations to conference-style meetings. As a result, account managers now capitalize on the group dynamics and have interactive meetings with short presentations and heavy discussion.

The key to highly participative group discussions is effective use of questions to get the conversation going and to keep it flowing.

By using three types of "consensus questions" (aimed at different people) significant feedback (and results!) can be accomplished. For example, reinforcement questions are directed at the receptive leader (you want him or her to do most of the talking to influence the peer group) and supporters. (Example: "That's an interesting point. What impact will it have on profits?") You can also ask testimony questions of the expert(s) to surface predictable positive answers. (Example: "Alice, can you explain how our software will enhance communications?") Finally, understanding questions are used to check feedback to make sure everyone is on the same page. (Example: "Alice, does this change make sense for your operation? Are you comfortable with it?")

While other elements of the presentation are important, identifying the receptive leader (and other roles) is essential, and planning the appropriate questions are musts for the key sales call in team selling. A sample key sales call organizer is in Exhibit 2.3. As you'll see, it covers most of the bases and leaves little room for error or surprises.

The key sales call in team selling is the moment of truth. It is the ultimate tactical opportunity for landing the big sale, but only if the other important strategic steps or tactics leading up to this group presentation have been taken; it's where battles are won or lost. Consider the sales team that worked hard for many months to set up a key sales call but didn't do all the necessary detective work. In the middle of their key sales call, an executive showed up late. He was briefly introduced by name and, after the sales team continued for a half hour, he abruptly departed. Ultimately, he turned out to be the final decision maker, and the deal went to a competitor. The competitor correctly identified the ultimate decision maker (leader) and apparently got him to participate in its presentation.

◇ Tactic 6: Execute Follow-up

This is a final tactic and it relates back to Selling 101. Individual follow-up sales calls are often needed as part of the team selling process. The follow-up may include additional key sales calls as well. The strategy may still be evolving after the first key sales call and will often require team members to follow up personally or make phone contact. Depending on the results of the key sales call, the process may be repeated. Anyone who has been in the sales "trenches" recently knows that many organizations go through eliminations, asking for repeat presentations, ultimately narrowing the "cattle calls" down to a few competitors in a "finalist presentation."

Regardless of the situation, team selling and team utilization is a critical ability in today's marketplace, and any manager or salesperson who sees these key presentations as a single event is in big trouble. Team selling, as a strategy, mandates a great deal of planning and scheming and weeks, even months, to initiate and complete the mission. As in sports such as football or baseball, tactics and skills are vital, but it's the preparation and strategy implementation that usually make the difference for the winner.

E X H I B I T   2 . 3   Sample Key Sales Call Organizer

Major steps	Directed to:	Presented by:	Supported with:
1. Lead-in *Intro's*	All four	Ellen	
Objective: Agree to 1st shipment/trial			Flipchart
Benefit: greatly enhanced efficiency/cost reduction			
Provide agenda.			Agenda
2. Update		Ellen	
Review conversations in preliminary calls	A. Richardson		Handout
Rationale: to allow all key people to make their decision	B. Robbins		
3. Presentation outline			
Benefits—features:			
Competetitive cost (we're 15% lower)	D. Sims	Ed	Cost chart
	A. Richardson		
Flexibility of payment	A. Richardson	Ellen	
Product specifications	B. Robbins	Ed	Technical
(They match or beat Empire in all areas)			Manual
- power efficiency			Experts
- output capacity			
- no need to reload after initial start-up			
4. Consensus questions			
1) Ask Richardson about his colleagues' comments (they were favorable)	A. Richardson	Bob	
2) After Ed presents all specs, ask Robbins, "You Agree the features are on par or better than the competition?"	B. Robbins	Ellen/Ed	
5. Close	D. Sims & A. Richardson	Ellen	Delivery schedule
Ask if we can schedule first shipment in 2 weeks			

3

C H A P T E R

Consultative
Selling Strategy

THE MYSTERY OF CONSULTATIVE SELLING

Consultative selling, a powerful strategy that can generate major results, is arguably the most difficult and challenging strategy to execute. Even the definition of consultative selling and the manner in which it is carried out are often difficult to comprehend. For example, start with the word *consultant*. The dictionary defines a consultant as "a person who gives expert and professional advice." That in itself is simple. It should be every salesperson's dream job description. However, when we combine selling with consulting (consultative selling), the job description becomes more complicated; if giving expert and professional advice were all that consultative selling required, we could skip this chapter.

The challenge (and mystery) of consultative selling is positioning yourself so you can become an expert on more complex problems than your company's products and more valuable to the account(s). It's expected that salespeople bring expertise on their products, services, and applications. The challenge of consultative selling is (1) building on that expertise to consult on broader account problems and (2) being proactive in your consultative approach. Consultative selling strategy is a process that requires the sales professional to initiate, pursue, and manage from one level to another, and even to know when to abort a specific mission. The strategy, as you'll learn, is implemented in low gear initially, with a

limited number of accounts and prospects. However, when a suitable opportunity is discovered, the strategy is accelerated to new levels of pursuit; at this point, the salesperson should focus and only execute this
strategy with one or two accounts at a time.

The consultative selling strategy *requires* expertise, professionalism, and consulting skills. It is a strategy that must be learned, and it is
one that needs time to implement. As a strategy, it can differentiate you
from the competition, build long-range relationships, and earn credibility
with specific accounts. Most important, it will enable you to penetrate
high-potential accounts by exceeding their expectations. However, you
should recognize that it's much more than being "consultative." Consultative selling strategy is a discipline that may take months or years to
generate results, but when it works, it succeeds big time: major orders,
repeat business, account respect and loyalty, penetration beyond belief. If
you're selling to complex, high-potential accounts or prospects, are willing to enhance your selling skills and knowledge, and have the discipline
to execute a long-term strategy, this one is for you. This chapter will re-
move the mystery of consultative selling and provide you with the tools
to execute it.

WHAT IS CONSULTATIVE SELLING STRATEGY?

In brief, consultative selling strategy establishes a "temporary partnership" in solving account problems. It requires a series of proactive tactics
designed to uncover problems that the account may not be aware of, has
not been able to solve, or does not understand the effect they're having
on business and profits. The ultimate objective of the consultative selling
strategy is to "partner" with the account in solving problems in customer
operations where you have a joint stake. It's important to recognize that
consultative selling goes beyond product selling. In the short run, the
problem you identify (and solve) may not even involve your product or
service, but it does reside in operations where your product/service is
used or resold. In other words, you use your expertise and knowledge of
the customer's operations to provide efficiency, improve sales, eliminate
bottlenecks, and in the long term generate profits. The solution to the account's problem(s) may involve your product directly or it may not. The
payback for you and your company is increased credibility, future sales
opportunities, improved relationships, visibility, trust, and status as a

"consultant," rather than as a look-alike vendor. All these rewards add up to more sales, of course, either immediately (as part of the solution) and certainly in the long term as a respected member of the account's team.

The consultative selling strategy goes beyond problems that your products/services can solve; it focuses on areas where your products/services are used, stored, or handled and includes related departments and functions. Since you have the expertise in product application and normally have access to these areas, you simply expand your knowledge and skills to search for problems and opportunities. Here's how.

 **CASE STUDY**

CONSULTATIVE SELLING STRATEGY IN ACTION

Following are examples of how the consultative selling strategy works:

- A grocery products account manager visits retail chain outlets and identifies an ongoing out-of-stock problem involving her products and the competition's as well. With the help of account headquarters staff, she broadens her study to more stores, defines the scope and cost of the problem in terms of lost sales, and enables the account to (1) restock shelves with the most profitable products (both hers and the competition's) and (2) increase inventory on fast-moving items. Chain profits increase.

- A paper products salesperson, visiting a printing plant on a regular basis, observes that the account is having consistent downtime due to breakdown/repairs on equipment. He teams up with the plant manager to provide data that pinpoints a 10 percent productivity loss. Together they determine that new equipment will pay for itself (by eliminating downtime and increasing production) in two years and persuade management to make the purchase.

- A temporary-staffing-services sales rep, working with a high-potential, fast-growing account, while satisfied to be the number one supplier with a major share of the business, is concerned that the account is adding new vendors and diluting quality. Focusing on the quality that the account is receiving, the sales rep works with

CASE STUDY c o n t i n u e d

needed). Eventually, the sales rep persuades the account to "partner" with her and outsource the entire temp operation to her company, thus enabling them to provide temps directly or go to competitive temp companies on a select basis.

- An auto parts salesperson selling to distributors, while traveling with distributors' salespeople, recognizes a variety of sales problems. The highest priority is call allocation among accounts, and it is apparent that most of the salespeople call on their accounts, regardless of potential, with the same frequency. Subsequently, he persuades the distributor sales manager to provide training on territory management (allocating calls according to account potential) with a resulting sales increase of 20 percent across all product lines.

The common denominator for these diverse situations, customers, and industries is the consultative selling strategy: identifying a problem or opportunity and partnering with the account to solve the problem or capitalize on the opportunity, while improving customer profits. The bottom line is that it works in every industry.

YOU WIN EVEN WHEN CONSULTATIVE SELLING DOESN'T WORK

The consultative selling strategy takes time to work and should be focused on high-potential accounts only. Like prospecting, it is, to a certain degree, a "numbers game." You won't necessarily find a problem or opportunity in every account, and you certainly won't find it immediately. Even if you do, the account may decide to ignore the problem or solve it in its own way. As a result, you may have to abort the strategy at an early stage. The good news is that no company ever operates at 100 percent efficiency because of growth, personnel problems, unawareness, poor training, operational problems, and so on. There are *always* ways to improve the efficiency (and profitability) of most departments and operations.

As you'll discover, consultative selling is an ongoing strategy that can be employed in all major accounts. Because of the long "sales" cycle (to identify the problem/opportunity and get a solution implemented), as well as the extra time and effort involved on your part, you may think, "Why bother?" since you are risking valuable time and focus. However, it is a no-risk situation that not only provides significant benefits to you and the account, if you hit pay dirt, but provides fallout benefits in every case:

- You get in-depth knowledge of the account, various players, the core of their business operations, their culture, their needs, and their problems. *As a result, you will sell the account more effectively!*
- You will earn greater respect and trust and improve relationships. Not only will the account decision makers appreciate your interest and professionalism, but they also will perceive you as a unique resource. *As a result, you will sell the account more effectively!*

RED FLAG

CONSULTATIVE SELLING STRATEGY IS NOT PRODUCT SELLING

Above all, consultative selling is not product or application selling. Following are a few key points of distinction:

- Product selling focuses on the product: features, benefits, performance, pricing, and so on. The need for the product is usually apparent to the account and forms the main foundation for the selling story. Other business opportunities are not generally called to the account's attention. Consultative selling focuses on the applications for the product and the account's business opportunities, which may or may not be apparent to the account, and develops them further, allowing the account to capitalize on the opportunity.
- Product selling requires the salesperson to stay within the traditional spheres of selling influence and take a straightforward approach to the needs of the decision maker and account. Consultative selling requires the salesperson to go beyond the traditional spheres of selling influence and to look closely at the account organization and operation.
- In product selling, the product normally provides the immediate solution to an account's needs. In consultative selling, the product or service may or may not be part of the immediate solution. Because the account generally views opportunity situations as "problems," what the salesperson will sell to the account is a "solution"— actually a means of exploiting those opportunities to increase the account's profitability.

OVERVIEW OF THE CONSULTATIVE SELLING STRATEGY MODEL

Exhibit 3.1 is a graphic of the consultative selling model, which contains six steps, or tactics. In practice, some of these tactics may overlap or even change in sequence. However, none should be skipped or circumvented.

EXHIBIT 3.1

Consultative Selling Model

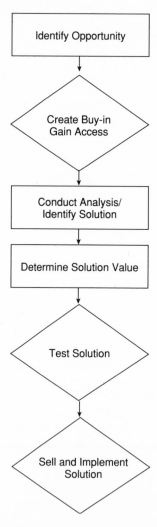

As mentioned in Chapter 1, a strategy is a series of tactics, actions, and steps. The first tactic in the consultative selling strategy is *identify the opportunity.* This can be implemented with almost any account and it is a structured (preferably) or casual search for opportunities (problems within the account). Since you have access to your accounts, you observe the departments you visit on regular calls and those related to where your products are used.

Create buy-in/gain access is a second tactic, and you move to this level only when you discover an opportunity or problem worth pursuing. Once you find a possible opportunity, it behooves you to accelerate the consulting process and find a "champion" who understands the potential rewards of solving the problem and will help you gain access to other people or information needed to pursue it.

The third tactic, or step, in the model is *conduct analysis/identify solution.* This requires detective work to analyze the problem, pinpoint the cause, and come up with an adequate solution or menu of options.

The fourth tactic, *determine solution value,* is a critical step. Since you are normally dealing with an intangible problem, or opportunity, the value of the solution needs to be determined in projected dollars saved, profits, or future benefits, along with the cost of implementation: a benefit/cost proposal.

Test solution, the fifth tactic, is a safety step to ensure that the solution will work and is the best option.

Finally, in step six, you help *sell and implement the solution.* This tactic should come naturally because it capitalizes on traditional (and professional!) selling skills.

The "boxed" tactics in Exhibit 3.1 require research and analysis, whereas the diamond-shaped ones involve face-to-face selling situations with the account. One consultative selling strategy challenge is the need to shift gears between both types of skills. This factor, coupled with the long sales cycle, make discipline, tools, and focus imperative to successful implementation. Here's how the tactics work together to form a synergistic strategy that can produce a huge payback.

☐ Tactic 1: Identify the Opportunity

Like most first steps, this is the toughest one, but not because it's difficult to get started. The difficulty is in continuing after the start, searching for a problem or opportunity that may *not* exist. In some ways, the first step in the consultative selling strategy is like prospecting for gold with no guarantee of a tangible reward for the effort and certainly no payback in the short term. The objective of the first step is to find a potential opportunity or problem, *not* to solve it.

As indicated, the consultative salesperson is a problem solver in search of opportunities. This takes time and continuity; it must be developed into a routine investigation each time the salesperson visits the customer headquarters or facilities. You may have to stretch your search beyond your decision-maker's facility and visit operations where your products are stored and used. Extra time is not required, but consistent observation, probing, and learning are musts for every sales call.

You may ask: "Why is a salesperson better qualified to solve problems than the account's own staff?" First, an outsider can be more objective and can provide a fresh, unbiased, nonpolitical view of operations. Second, you possess specific expertise to focus on the problem or opportunity: application knowledge as well as familiarity with the arena where the product or service is used (production, office, warehouse, finance, retail/distributor outlet). Third, you should be more motivated to capitalize on the opportunity than the account employee. Fourth, most salespeople have or can gain access to areas where their products are used and to the people who use them. Fifth, you have an opportunity for continual learning about your accounts' operations. Consequently, you bring a special focus to bear on that department every time you visit it. Sixth, and most important, you have the selling skills to cut through the bureaucracy and sell the concept at different levels in the account organization.

For example, a salesperson selling packaging machinery should know or learn a great deal about production: cycle time, just-in-time inventory, statistical process control, and so on. Similarly, a grocery-products salesperson knows the ins and outs of the retail-food chain: ROS (return on space), traffic flow patterns, pricing, category management, and so forth. A banker certainly knows cash flow, asset management, how to leverage financing, and more.

At this professional level you can put the knowledge to work to enhance the customer's profit: increased sales and more efficient operating costs. Every customer has a myriad of problems, inefficiencies, and unfulfilled goals, and each one needs expert help. Since few salespeople instinctively do consultative selling you need a strategy to make the process second nature. While most salespeople are occasionally presented with consultative opportunities, the consultative selling strategy has more impact if you proactively use it and search for opportunities.

I D E A

USE AN OPPORTUNITY ANALYSIS TOOL

One tool that is helpful to the consultative selling strategy, particularly in the discovery step (*identify the opportunity*), is an opportunity analysis checklist that serves as (1) a track to run on, what and where to look for opportunities, and (2) a reminder that *every time* you visit a customer you should be searching for opportunities. An example of a checklist appears in Exhibit 3.2. This example is used by consumer packaged goods key account managers when visiting grocery retail stores and headquarters. It's a worksheet to help zero in on problems or opportunities.

The opportunity analysis worksheet breaks down the operating area that the consultative salesperson normally has access to such as departments, resources (equipment and inventory), work spaces, or operations. These are called opportunity areas. Within each area are opportunity indicators—specific, quantifiable, or observable factors that often point out opportunities for improved efficiency, faster turnover, increased sales, cost savings, better quality, or for solving repetitive problems or those caused by change. The grid customizes and simplifies their search and acts as an ongoing "shopping list." When a potential area problem is spotted, the account manager shifts gears to the oportunity idicators column and searches for possible causes.

The ultimate search may uncover a potential opportunity that has nothing to do with your product or service; of course, it can relate directly to *increased* product use also. Even in the former case, there's usually a significant payback when the solution is implemented. It comes in terms of improved relationships, confidence, respect, and goodwill, all of which ultimately translate into more business for the consultative salesperson who provides these benefits.

◇ Tactic 2: Create Buy-in—Gain Access

Generally, it's easy to accomplish this tactic and doesn't take much time—perhaps a sales call or two on key decision makers or those who can help the salesperson gain access to additional information. At this early stage in the process, you will seldom have enough information to fully and specifically define the problem/opportunity. To facilitate this step, you should utilize your selling skills to communicate the opportunity and to sell the decision maker on partnering the solution. You need to

E X H I B I T   3.2

Opportunity Analysis Worksheet for Consumer Package Goods

1. Product distribution	■ Range ■ Mix ■ Gaps ■ Private label vs. brand name
2. Inventory optimization	■ Turnover ■ Out-of-stocks ■ Backroom-to-shelf movement
3. Space management	■ Allocation by market share ■ DPP/ROI ■ Allocation vs. other categories
4. Shelf location	■ Split/single ■ Traffic flow ■ Aisle neighbors
5. Merchandising	■ Payback ■ Special displays ■ Shelf maintenance planogram ■ Pricing ■ POS materials
6. Advertising	■ Display and TV ■ Coupons ■ Circulars ■ Response rate
7. Store image	■ Super store, food, specialty, upscale ■ Customer base/demographics ■ Layout/size/condition ■ Store locations
8. Customer personnel	■ Adequately staffed ■ Training needs ■ Efficient/courteous
9. Order/payment processing	■ Order entry procedure ■ Optimized order size/timing/method of delivery ■ Cash flow
10. Direct procesing costs	■ Warehousing costs ■ Store delivery costs ■ Case pack/inner pack costs ■ In-store handling costs
11. Pricing	■ Parity ■ Advantage/disadvantage ■ Pricing strategy
12. Category management	■ Full/partial concept ■ Concept working ■ Achieving profit objectives

CASE STUDY

IDENTIFY OPPORTUNITY TACTIC

Let's examine an example of the first step in the consultative selling strategy. A salesperson for an overseas freight forwarding company, which provides shipping tankers for Europe and Australia, periodically visits a client's loading dock to observe container loading procedures. While he can make on-the-spot recommendations to the customer on what loading equipment is most effective, he also inspects the various types of cargo, looking for potential problems (shifting weight, packaging, efficient loading, etc.)

One commodity the customer ships frequently is plastic rolls in "standard" lengths. When stacked on end, they leave a 12-inch space in the top of the container. This is not a significant loss of space by any means, and the salesperson quickly estimates the cost of the space lost per container to be around $400; not much of a savings if this were only a random shipment for this plastic. However, he quickly realizes this commodity and these specific-size rolls are the bulk of this particular customer's shipments.

At this point in the consultative selling process, he's uncovered a potential opportunity in search of a solution, and it may have significant payback for the customer. If so, there are three possible solutions: fill the space with other products, stack the merchandise differently, or change the length of the plastic rolls to utilize 100 percent of the space. He's now ready for the next tactic or step in the consultative selling strategy, and so are you. The case study will continue later.

ask "consulting-type" questions designed to make the decision maker aware of the problem/opportunity and get him or her to "buy in" and support the quest for a solution. Failure to get buy-in from the right people might be the first signal to abort the project. This tactic is a selling scenario. For most salespeople who recognize the importance and focus of this step, it's usually accomplished without great difficulty. While the key objective is to test interest and build support (finding a champion for the project), there are other needs.

Often, access to specific data, people, and locations is required, so the added objective for this call (or calls) is to get permission to identify and interview personnel, observe account operations, and check facts, figures, and projections.

As indicated earlier, even if you abort this particular consultative selling mission (for whatever reason) you benefit. Your investment of time has provided access to other decision makers and influencers within the account and exposure to account problems. This is a significant benefit to any smart salesperson.

 I D E A

USE CONSULT QUESTIONS

You can create buy-in effectively by using "consult" questions. These are questions designed to lead the customer to an awareness of the problem and a commitment to pursue a solution. The four types of consult questions, which work best in this sequence, are:

- *Status questions*—uncover facts about the *current situation* in the account (questions requiring answers the decision makers can give you easily, without thinking about it too hard).

    —What is the current out-of-stock situation?

    —How many people work in the department?

    —On average, how much time is spent rating a typical insurance policy?

    —Is production downtime occurring?

- *Attitude questions*—uncover *feelings* about the current status and reveal to you areas of dissatisfaction or difficulty. Attitude questions let you know how much work you have to do. If, for example, you see an opportunity to improve results, but attitude questions reveal the account doesn't see it that way, then you know you'll have to develop that opportunity a lot further in his or her mind. It's the old story of how people won't do anything about a problem until they actually see it as a problem, it becomes a problem for them, or the opportunity leaps at them.Status and attitude questions help you figure out where the account is in relation to a given problem or opportunity.

    —How do you think the out-of-stock situation affects your profitability on a local store level?

    —Would you say your staff is overworked?

    —Do you think that's an inordinate amount of time to spend on just one policy?

IDEA c o n t i n u e d

—How does management feel about the downtime?

■ *Consequence questions*—help the account to consider the results or consequences of a problem or opportunity; expand or increase the importance of a problem/opportunity in the mind of the account and thus build a sense of urgency.

—Have you ever considered what a chronic out-of-stock situation means in terms of lost sales over the course of a year?

—How does the staffing situation affect your ability to package and produce orders?

—If they weren't taking all that time handling policy paperwork, how else might your agents be spending their time?

—Isn't repetitive downtime an expensive problem?

■ *Value questions*—help define the value of the solution to the account and explore the account's benefits from capitalizing on the opportunity. An important feature of the consultative selling strategy is that the solution you ultimately come up with should be stated in terms of value to the account. These questions will help you establish the value of your solution in the account's mind at an early stage.

—How would eliminating this out-of-stock situation affect your stores' profitability?

—What would happen if you were able to hire temporary workers to fill the gaps left in the staff?

—How many more premiums could you realize if your agents were able to spend 30 percent more of their time acquiring new policyholders?

—What financial impact would the elimination of downtime have?

These types of questions help you explore all the opportunity areas and opportunity indicators in your accounts. Ideally, the consult questions should move in sequence from status to value. If you follow this sequence, you start with easy questions and move gradually to tougher, more penetrating issues.

The objective of this questioning technique is to make the accounts recognize and think about opportunities they may never have considered before, to consider what the consequences of solving or not solving a problem might be, and to begin to define what the value of a solution would be to them.

A second objective is to create buy-in in the mind of the account. Consult questions cause the account decision makers to realize there is something they need to think about—with your help. So while you are asking consult questions, you are also creating buy-in for your approach. The buy-in you create increases your chances of gaining the access you need to pursue the solution.

While discovering a problem/opportunity is the foundation for consultative selling, asking effective consult questions is the heart of the strategy.

☐ Tactic 3: Conduct Analysis—Identify Solution

Depending on the type of problem/opportunity, you may have to do some analysis to pinpoint the scope and help identify the best solution. This will require collecting information to generate solution options. Data may be available or you may have to create your own through observation, asking questions, or possibly doing other types of research.

For most consultative types of problems, you need to focus on specifics and ask yourself these questions:

- What is the scope of the problem?
- Is it affecting other processes or departments?
- How often is this problem/situation occurring?
- What possible costs are involved (people, equipment, inventories, time, etc.)?
- What is causing the problem or creating the opportunity?
- What options are available for eliminating this problem or improving this situation?
- What is the best solution?

The objective of this step or tactic is to help define how serious the problem/opportunity is, what the potential payback (profit, sales, efficiency) might be, and most important, what are the likely solutions. Here's an example, from the case study scenario.

☐ Selling Tactic 4: Determine Solution Value

The objective of this step is to quantify the solution so that the opportunity can be presented in specific, measurable terms. While the benefit of taking action (getting the solution implemented) may be obvious to account deci-

CASE STUDY

CONDUCT ANALYSIS—IDENTIFY SOLUTION

The freight forwarding salesperson in the example cited earlier found it necessary to meet with the account's traffic manager and the plant manager. Once he got buy-in from the purchasing agent (his normal contact) he met with the other decision makers to pursue the best option and to collect supporting data. He had to check on current and future shipments of plastics to the ports his organization served, and he needed data on all available sizes, total shipments of each, as well as the feasibility of changing roll sizes if needed. This mission required two sales calls and a half-day reviewing his data and notes. At this point, it seemed feasible to change roll sizes at the production level without major costs and without affecting the needs or applications of existing users of the plastic. The salesperson saw this as the obvious solution, and now he had to determine what the realistic savings might be if this course of action were implemented. He was ready for the next step or tactic.

sion-makers, it may also fall short. In today's marketplace, with committees prevailing along with multiple decision-makers and the focus on dollar values, it's essential that the consultative salesperson reinforce his/her recommendations with hard numbers. The "consultant" can't wait for the account to determine the savings or calculate the projected returns; you must do it yourself. Therein lies the importance of this step.

Before presenting the concept to account management, it's necessary to put a tangible value on the solution. In some instances, the data may be available from previous steps, but in most instances, it will require some creative number-crunching and a keen assessment of the solution parameters. To facilitate this number-crunching and to maximize the ultimate number, utilize the QLP formula, which, simply stated, says quantify the various indicators, link them together to maximize the payback, and project the value of the solution over time to make it even more significant.

Quantify the solution by expressing it in specific, measurable terms, such as:

- Time
- Labor
- Dollars
- Accuracy rates

- Operating efficiencies
- Projected sales or profit increases.

Link the various opportunity areas and indicators that arise. Frequently, these indicators will interact to provide a more favorable business payback. By linking several opportunity indicators, it's possible to establish an even greater value for the solution in the mind of the customer. Finally, project the value of the solution to make it even more apparent and significant to the customer.

There are many opportunities for projecting the values, and it can be done in different ways. Value can be projected over time—a year, three years, or longer, depending on what's a realistic period over which to extrapolate savings, project sales, or amortize costs. The value can be projected in terms of numbers of units: stores, workstations, installations, departments, and so on.

The value can also be projected over the number of people involved. For example, one consultative salesperson discovered a step-elimination savings in "finishing" a product in the one factory located in his territory. However, he quickly realized that the identical savings could be achieved by eliminating the same step in 10 other factories in different areas and projected the savings accordingly.

How the consultative salesperson determines the solution value will vary from situation to situation. But keep in mind and use (or learn) the following tools and methods, which pertain to different options:

Return on investment: cost or yield on equipment, purchases, use of space, inventory turnover, and so on.

Inventory expense: should be minimized because it always ties up dollars.

Resources: people, time, and space—all these cost money and will increase profits when used or employed efficiently.

Equipment: expensive to maintain and operate and should be amortized to illustrate annual costs. You can also measure its productivity by units produced or processed.

Money: also a cost factor; when money is involved, show the value of discounts and interest rates.

Sales forecasts: very persuasive when discussing potential sales increases; always include sales forecasts in the solution, along with the costs and profits of achieving them.

An infinite number of tools is available to quantify, link, and project solutions. It's a must to keep current with new methods for measuring the performance of operations in accounts. The consultative selling approach mandates that the salesperson be an expert in each customer's business. That's what a partnership is all about!

 I D E A

INCLUDE COST OF IMPLEMENTATION

The final objective of determining the solution value is to compare it to the cost of implementation. Because solutions often require some kind of change—a change in procedures, equipment, personnel, or improved systems— it will probably require some kind of cost to the account. To convince the account that the solution value overrides the solution cost, use the QLP formula to compute the cost of implementation and compare it with the long-term benefits.

 **C A S E   S T U D Y**

DETERMINE SOLUTION VALUE

Consider again the example of the freight forwarding salesperson who uncovered an opportunity for optimizing his customer's container space. He knew that to motivate the necessary executives in the account to change the length of the plastic rolls, he had to show significant savings. He had determined that this option was the best one because it was feasible (without extra manufacturing cost or inconvenience to customers), but it would involve time, effort, and a commitment to make the change. Consequently, he realized he had to put a value on the end result. The actual savings per shipping container (gained by filling dead space with product) was $421 per container. Based on about 100 containers being shipped per year, an annual savings/return benefit of $42,100 was revealed. When projected over three years, a reasonable assumption, the value became a very significant $126,300. When compared with the $5,000 die costs involved, the value remained significant. Needless to say, he got the project completed and enjoyed the rewards: credibility from the account plus a growing share of the client's shipping business.

◇ Tactic 5: Test the Solution

The fifth tactic or step in the consultative selling model is to test the solution. It is a pivotal step because it is the first opportunity to begin "selling" the solution recommendations. Taking this step provides many advantages; you can't afford to skip it or take it lightly. You can accomplish this step by having the customer verify your calculations, by conducting a test (such as a sample run or pilot), or by running the concept by various decision makers at the account for their input.

This tactic enables you to:

- Verify what's happening in the decision process. This step helps cover all the bases and ensures that every important decision maker and influencer in the decision loop has been included.
- Uncover other needs or a hidden agenda of the customer. When conducting the test, the customer may think up new ways to use the solution or may reveal ideas that he or she never discussed before.
- Broaden the sphere of influence. In solution testing, the account will almost certainly draw other people into the process. This allows you to influence their thinking about the solution and build support.
- Stay close to the customer. Testing means additional involvement with the customer. It allows you to get a strong grip on the customer's working environment;—it lets the customer feel that the salesperson is heavily involved in the operation and cares deeply about the outcome of the solution. It enhances the partnership aspect of consultative selling.
- Reinforce the account's participation. This step allows the customer to refine the recommendation. The initial recommendation isn't always going to be perfect; testing allows him or her to fine-tune it to the realities of the organization. This step also buttresses the account's sense of ownership of the solution.

◇ Tactic 6: Sell the Solution

The sixth and final tactic in the consultative selling model may be the easiest of all to implement—if you have taken all the previous steps carefully and successfully. Even though this step calls for selling skills acquired through experience, you can't leave anything undone. In other words, if you have come this far, at considerable expense of time and effort, you must plan the final step carefully to guarantee a payback for the effort. Most of the action steps involved in selling the solution are of the checklist variety—questions, reminders, and planning tips.

The objective of solution selling is to maximize previous information gathered in the earlier phases of consultative selling and leverage that information with the final decision maker(s) in the account.

Successful solution selling occurs when you can answer "yes" to these questions:

- Has adequate research and analysis been done?
- Have all questions been asked and answered?
- Have all values been defined?
- Is the account in agreement with the "test" solution?
- Is presentation of the solution to the final decision makers the only step left?

No matter what form the preliminary work has taken, always consider the following:

The solution selling step is when all of the ultimate decision makers should be on hand. If the final decision makers have not been present up to this point, the audience for this step will be different than it has been. Include supportive people from the account, as well as a limited number of people who contributed to the result. The solution selling step is the time to call in your company's resources. These may include corporate executives, technical experts or specialists, and anyone who can enhance your recommendations with know-how, rank, and credibility. Your resources may also mean compiling graphics, prototype packages, slide presentations, or whatever else is necessary to sell your solution persuasively.

The solution selling step should include a management summary, preferably in writing. Whether presented in writing or verbally/visually, the summary should follow this content outline: the objective of your consultative approach, description of research and analysis methods, summary of findings, and recommendations.

The consultative selling strategies require your involvement throughout the implementation period. Remember, the account has "bought" because you, as the consultant, created the need. It's important to reinforce the account's decision by having the salesperson stay visible and accessible. The sales consultant's presence during implementation establishes continuity and nourishes the long-term partnership—the main objective of consultative selling. It also keeps the door open for regular or additional business. You can stay involved during the implementation of the solution through transition meeting(s), ongoing coordination, periodic check-ins, telephone contacts, interim reviews, measuring of results, and "spreading the word."

In the final analysis, the consultative selling strategy is a paradox of sorts. It's one of the most powerful and effective strategies, yet it's the most challenging to implement. However, with proper direction, discipline, tools, and careful account targeting, it can be a major force for account penetration, development, management, and maintenance. And, as stated earlier, even if it doesn't work to completion, you still gain in terms of account knowledge, trust, relationship, and professionalism.

4
C H A P T E R

"Selling" Value-Added Services Strategy

HOW VALUE-ADDED STRATEGY DIFFERENTIATES YOU FROM THE COMPETITION

If you are concerned about differentiating yourself from the competition, this is the strategy for you. Regardless of whether you sell a commodity, a "look-alike" product or service, or an exclusive product (It won't be *exclusive* for long!), the value-added services strategy can help you differentiate yourself, your company, and your product offering. As you might imagine, this is *not* a one-shot tactic; it's a series of moves over time that are required to affect the customer's perception of your offering. The value-added services strategy requires creativity and patience, but when implemented effectively, it will position you and your company as a vendor that is different, and one that truly focuses on customer satisfaction.

According to Theodore Levitt, an acclaimed marketing guru of the Harvard Business School, there is no such thing as a commodity. Levitt claims in his book, *The Marketing Imagination:* "All goods and services can be differentiated and usually are. Though the usual presumption is that this is true more of consumer goods than of industrial goods and services, the opposite is the actual case." He goes on to explain that the only exceptions to this thinking are in the minds of people who profess these exceptions.

In other words, differentiation is everywhere because manufacturers, wholesalers, retailers, and sellers can and do add differentiation at various levels. Everyone wants his or her offering to be special, even companies that deal in pure commodities: produce, cement, steel, grain, chemicals, plastics, and, yes, even money.

The value-added services strategy is a "pure" approach because it relates indirectly to the selling of your products or services. It's a strategy that enables you to *differentiate*, and, it is hoped, distance yourself and your company from the competition. The strategy, as we will define it, enables you to capitalize on the services that your organization has developed as marketing tools to either differentiate itself or market its product/service more effectively. These services are usually given away. (The number of free services that your company provides is awesome, as you'll find out.) Together with your own creativity in providing customer service, they offer a powerful strategy for selling. Obviously, the value-added services overlap with other direct product/service selling efforts. Look at this strategy as an opportunity to position yourself and your organization, and as a vehicle for underlining the differences between your product/service offering and that of the competition. Does this sound like selling a concept? That's what the value-added benefits are all about: getting a ROI (return on investment) from the many value-added services that your company provides to customers. Before we get to the strategy, it's important to first understand the value-added concept and what it is.

WHAT "VALUE-ADDED" REALLY MEANS

One of the jargon complexities of recent times is the expression "value-added." It means different things to different people. For example:

- To a value-added reseller in the computer business, it means reselling computers (purchased from a manufacturer) and adding value via consulting, software, training, and other services, often packaged into one selling price.
- To a business forms/systems manufacturer, the value-added concept involves the salesperson's ability to do a comprehensive survey or study of a customer's operations or needs and provide detailed recommendations (without cost).
- To many salespeople, and in our perception, value-added services are defined as the many types of services provided to customers

without cost. These value-added services range from samples to consulting, from data support to special payment terms, training, and more.

The common denominator for all three examples above is that the value-added services generate *extra benefits* and are provided *without cost* to the customer.

The value-added services that we deal with in this strategy can be provided by both the salesperson and the company; we'll talk more about that later. Some value-added services are permanent and offered to every customer, and others are special, to make a sale, to accommodate a special need, or simply to provide quality service and support. The bottom line is that these services are supplied largely without cost to the customer, but at significant cost to you and your company.

The concept behind the value-added strategy is using these values as a springboard for selling—communicating the *extra* values to the customer on an ongoing basis to build goodwill, to enhance your total offering, even to negotiate with. Since "selling" these value-added services involves a series of actions over time, value-added selling takes on the life of a full-blown strategy. Most important, it can be a powerful one, as evidenced by the following, real-world case study.

 CASE STUDY

Before we move to the process steps for executing the value-added services strategy (i.e., selling value-added services), here's an example of how one major company used this strategy to differentiate itself from its competition.

Brand G, as we'll call the company, is a major producer of gelatin capsules. Its major customers are the pharmaceutical and over-the-counter manufacturers of drugs and vitamins. While the end product is a high-tech capsule, provided in custom design with huge volume potential, it is nevertheless considered by most buyers to be a commodity. After all, the same gelatin is used to manufacture competitive products, and similar sophisticated equipment generates the end units in millions. What's more, the industry has been driven to impose annual contracts, which become the source of intense negotiations between buyers and sellers.

CASE STUDY continued

Despite this, Brand G has managed to (1) maintain the highest level of pricing in the industry and (2) build a 50 percent market share! Selling value-added services cannot take sole credit for this remarkable feat, but it is an important strategy that fits into and reinforces the company's intensive marketing and sales efforts. Here's how.

Brand G is well managed and the marketing effort, by design, has evolved an extensive menu of value-added services for its customers. Included in its list of services (provided without cost) are tools like:

- Quality training seminars for customers.
- Parts replacement and service of customer filling/packaging equipment (most of the machines are custom made or imported, with poor service by original manufacturers and/or nonexistent parts).
- 800 telephone numbers for all customer service/order departments.
- Just-in-time inventory programs.
- Logo design for each new customer product.
- Special packaging for bulk shipments to customers.
- And so on, to over 50 different value-added services!

On a call I made with a Brand G salesperson, we chatted with the customer casually after the business issues were taken care of. When the opportunity surfaced, I asked the buyer for this major pharmaceutical company: "How do you perceive the value-added services that Brand G brings to your organization?"

The buyer digested the question and, after some thought, replied: "They provide value in a number of ways, but one minor example occurred recently when we launched our new allergy drug. You may not realize it, but every capsule has a miniature logo on it, which most companies fuss over and the FDA must approve. Typically, when we are getting ready to apply for FDA approval, which is a lengthy process, we submit the logo design. When the new drug was ready for submission to the FDA, we called in three gelatin capsule producers and asked them to come to a briefing and submit their logo designs. After the briefing, Brand G design engineers worked out the concept, developed some samples on their CadCam computers, and returned within a few days. One competitor

took about two weeks, another became an 'also-ran' when we hadn't received a response from them three weeks later! Because of the design and
fast response we selected Brand G's design."

I couldn't help but add: "So the benefit to you was that this value-
added service provided both convenience and savings in getting the logo
designed." "True," the buyer quickly added, "but the real benefit to us was
the time-saving advantage of getting FDA approval for the drug." He later
estimated that the company saved a month's time and, as a result, was
able to get the drug on the market a full month earlier.

Later, in reviewing this example of value-added service, it became apparent that the cost of providing this service was about $5,000 (for the de-
signers' time, CadCam equipment use, flight expense for customer brief-
ing/presentation), *but* the benefit to the customer in the first year
approximated $20 million in sales gain! This is what that *extra month of
selling time* was worth to the customer.

This is an unusual and rare example of the benefits provided by value-
added services. However, in most cases, the benefits are substantial.
Equally important, they are often tangible and the benefit expressed in
dollars becomes a forceful, persuasive, memorable selling tool for the
salesperson. That's what this strategy is all about. Value-added services
can have a dramatic impact on customer perception, loyalty, value, and
long-term relationships. The key to optimizing this strategy is: salespeople
identify value-added services and sell the true value to their customers

THE MODEL FOR EXECUTING THE VALUE-ADDED SERVICES STRATEGY

Every effective strategy needs a track to run on, to hold the strategy on
course over time. The strategic track for value-added selling involves a
series of tactics, some involving research and planning actions and others
requiring selling activities. In most instances, this strategy is implemented by the seller and the only resource that you need is a menu of
value-added services to draw on. We'll discuss that in more depth later.

EXHIBIT 4.1

"Selling" Value-Added Services Strategy Model

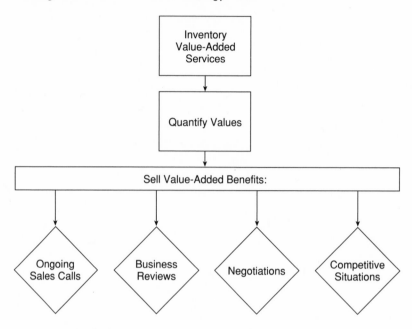

In Exhibit 4.1 you'll see a model of how the strategy is implemented. The model has a number of vertical steps, which eventually flow to a series of horizontal tactics. Let's overview the steps one at a time.

The first tactic, *inventory value-added services,* is taking inventory of the value-added services that your company already provides (has developed) and searching for personal services that you can add. Next, in the second tactic, *quantify values,* you "value" these services—determine which value is more significant, the estimated cost that your company (or you) has invested in each one, or the value of the benefit to the customer. Needless to say, the *value of the benefit* is usually significantly greater than the cost. Finally, we come to the selling tactics, *sell value-added benefits,* for which there are four basic selling "diamonds" of opportunity. You can use one or all; the more you build into the strategy, the more powerful is the end result. The four interacting and overlapping sales situation tactics are:

- *Ongoing sales calls*—using value-added benefits on most sales calls to set the stage for long-term payback.
- *Business reviews*—building in value-added services and benefits when you use this important selling presentation tool.
- *Negotiations*—offsetting customer demands using value-added services and their benefit to customers.
- *Competitive situations*—differentiating yourself from your competitors in head-to-head confrontations.

We'll cover these steps or tactics individually, as the strategy is described.

☐ Tactic 1: Inventory Value-Added Services

The challenge with identifying value-added services is that they have been developed or evolved piecemeal over time. As a result, the customers (and salespeople) take them for granted and they "lose their value" for both the customers and the sales organization. I recently attended a conference where one vendor demonstrated how it had set up a Web site for the Internet at considerable investment so its customers could actually interact with, or sample, various products. This is a state-of-the-art marketing tool that can provide great value (and benefits) to customers, but in time it will become an inventory item, be taken for granted, and literally lose its value to the seller.

You and your organization probably have 25 to 100 "taken-for-granted" value-added services sitting in inventory. Your company has spent thousands—probably millions—of dollars funding these services, yet they and you are not getting the ROI you deserve.

The first step is to do some creative thinking and/or research and inventory these items. This is basically a onetime step: once you develop a list of value-added services, you need only maintain it by adding new ones that your company develops, or ones that you yourself create. Some value-added services are broad based, available to any customer that needs them, while others are offered or used in the sales process for special situations or to meet the unique needs of certain customers. To help

EXHIBIT 4.2

Inventory of Value-Added Services

Support Services	Consulting Services
■ Training/education ■ Just-in-time delivery ■ Testing ■ Free service ■ Special terms or delivery ■ Safety programs ■ Action to build customer's business (coaching, advertising, etc)	■ Studies/research ■ Databases ■ On-site problem solving ■ Technical-service support ■ Quality studies and feedback ■ Product-design assistance ■ Quality improvement ■ Computer systems
Personal Services This category is reserved for value-added services that the salesperson provides: extra presentations, meetings, favors, executive overviews, business reviews, special projects, etc.	**Promotional Services** ■ Samples ■ Trials ■ Co-op advertising and promotion ■ Help in developing customer's business: mailings, referrals, etc. ■ Sales aids/tools ■ Customizing products ■ Brochures and literature

you focus your thinking, and to provide a frame of reference for inventorying value-added services, we've sorted them into four categories that appear in Exhibit 4.2. The categories, are unimportant and overlap, but they serve as a frame of reference to trigger the creation or identification of your own value-added services.

Support services are abundant in most organizations and can range from an 800 telephone number to elaborate (and expensive) services such as providing just-in-time delivery scheduling. Support services are generally the services your company makes available to all clients, and many of them become almost routine. For example, one of our clients, manufacturers of welding supplies, has set up elaborate tech centers around the country for training distributor personnel. The cost is huge, but the "free" benefits to customers are also significant. What support services does your organization provide that can be added to your value-added services inventory list?

Consulting services are similar to support services and their functions may overlap. However, the two can be viewed as separate entities, because consulting services are often people intensive and their services can be delivered in different ways for selected customers. They are often negotiated as part of the deal or to protect ongoing business. A good example of a consulting service is that supplied by major temporary personnel providers. For heavy-volume accounts, they have devised contracts and proposals that include placing their own managers on the client premises to manage the "outsourced" temp function. In other words, the temp provider organization handles a major segment of the client's temporary help by checking needs each day, selecting the temps, and even supervising them while on the job. In addition, they may provide their client with reports on quality of work performed by temps and jobs filled, along with timely recommendations on related issues. Think about the consulting services your company has developed and add them to your inventory.

Personal services are those the salesperson usually supplies on a personal basis or creates for the customer. Have you helped the customer solve problems, attended conventions (to maintain a sales booth), trained customer personnel, done special presentations, and so on? For example, in my first sales job with a major steel producer (selling stainless steel, a commodity), I was forced to be creative in order to differentiate what I was selling. I quickly discovered that our warehouse sheets of stainless steel, while specified and ordered by gauge (i.e., 24 gauge), had different tolerances, and a shipment of stainless steel would often be on the light or heavy side. For a customer who used 24-gauge stainless steel for nonstructural use (such as kitchen equipment), I could personally select those cases on the "light" side. Since stainless is expensive and sold by actual weight, this personal service saved selected accounts thousands of dollars each year. While I can't take credit for inventing value-added selling, this instinctive "value-added" strategy enabled me to build a strong client base in a short time.

The question you need to ask yourself is: What extra value have I provided in the past to different customers? Equally important, you should be asking: What other values can I provide, not only to serve the customer, but also to build an inventory of personal services?

Promotional services, as we label them, are more routine kinds of things you do for customers. Generally, these services are made available by you to help the customer's business grow (and, selfishly, sell your products). Services such as supplying samples, providing sales aids and tools, even customizing your products with special packaging or labels would certainly fall into this category.

As indicated, these four categories will overlap and the services that fall into each may look alike. Don't worry about the categories, per se. They've been included only to broaden your perspective and to trigger your creative juices into taking inventory of what present or potential value-added services you have available. In company seminars on value-added services that we conduct, it's rare to see a group of salespeople who can't brainstorm and identify at least 50 services that they presently, or could potentially, offer to customers—services that provide extra value without cost. Even 10 to 15 brainstormed items will arm you with an inventory of services to differentiate your products and company from the competition. We'll delve into this aspect of individualizing (and "selling") your value-added services later.

Once you've developed your inventory, you're ready to move to the next tactic: determining values for the most significant value-added services.

☐ Tactic 2: Quantify Values

Remember: all benefits are claims. As a result, benefits are intangible and sometimes difficult to grasp. When selling products or services, you use the features as a springboard in translating the benefits, and then back them up with proof, data, and sales aids. In presenting value-added benefits the benefit is even more intangible. It's 100 percent conceptual! The customer is usually not seeking it, or paying for it, and may not even comprehend it. In fact, there's usually a number of resources (services) that produce the value-added benefit. Because of this, it's essential to make the value-added benefit as concrete and tangible as possible, so you can present it effectively and the decision maker can both understand and appreciate it.

In quantifying value-added benefits, there are a few simple guidelines to remember:

- Not every value-added benefit can be quantified. Many value-added benefits, such as relationship, trust, "making someone look good," cannot be measured. However, keep in mind that most *value-added benefits can be quantified* with creativity and number crunching. Also, while all value-added benefits should be presented and reinforced, it's important to recognize that the ones that are quantified will be more visible and remembered longer. As a result, you will generate long-term sales and enhance relationships.

- When quantifying the value, *start with the value of the benefit,* and if you cannot measure it in specific terms, try to *compute the cost of the service* that provides the value-added benefit. For example, your company provides its customers with a safety training program (value-added service) and, while 200 of the account's plant personnel have completed the course, there's no way of measuring how much this has contributed to safety or a lower accident rate. However, with research, you can determine that a course like this would cost $500 if the account purchased it and can therefore value the benefit at $10,000 ($500 × 200 courses).

- When quantifying, try to *measure in bottom-line dollars:* profit increases, reduced overhead, increased productivity, and so on. While other measures such as percentages, numbers, days, tons, feet, are specific and measurable, dollars are more impressive, dramatic, and memorable. For example, it's more effective to say, "If you follow my inventory suggestion, you'll be able to generate a $20,000 annual return on the space saved," as compared to the less-effective statement, "You'll be able to find a more productive use for the 3,000 square feet saved by the inventory reduction."

- Often a number of *value-added services or benefits can be linked* to make a more sizable benefit. This is desirable to keep in mind when quantifying the total value-added contribution. Measure values piecemeal, but link them to increase the total amount of the benefits accruing to the customer.

- Finally, it's important to *project the values* over a longer period. Obviously, if a value-added benefit has a life cycle of six months or is a one-time enhancement, you are limited. However, if you provide an ongoing benefit to the customer, you have earned the right to value it over a longer period of time. Many salespeople use one to three years as a projection, but in the final analysis the projection must be (1) dictated by common sense, and (2) explained to the customer when you show him your projections. For example, it's more effective to say, "We estimated that our just-in-time delivery will save you $11,000 a year," rather than to say, "—will save you $300 each delivery."

 I D E A

USE IMPACT RESOURCES TO QUANTIFY VALUE-ADDED BENEFITS OF SERVICES

IMPACT is not a formula, but a method to help you include all the pertinent resources that go into providing value-added services or benefits.

The *I* in the acronym IMPACT stands for *inventory*. Some value-added services deliver inventory faster, help turn it over faster, require less space to sell or store it, or generate a higher return on the inventory investment. These inventory benefits can be measured independently or in concert with some of the other resources below. You should be aware of concepts, such as return on investment of inventory (and space), turnover, and just-in-time inventory. Use them in calculating savings and profits on inventory-driven value-added benefits.

The *M* in IMPACT refers to *money*. While money in itself (if used to measure increases in profits or sales, cost of assets, efficiencies, or savings) *is* a value, the money resource is also a reminder to add in the cost of money or, in banking terms, interest. For example, if your company saves an account $20,000 in inventory expense a year by storing the inventory yourself, you're justified in adding another $2,000 (i.e., 10 percent interest) on top. If the account had to invest that money, it would have to pay (or lose) interest. Remember, money is value, but the cost of money is important also.

The *P* represents the *people* resource, and this is an expensive enhancement. Always look for investment in people. Often, value-added benefits accomplish functions that the account's own staff would have to do; hence, *saving the account the cost of people* to perform those tasks. When calculating the cost of a person doing a task, add 25 percent to wages to cover fringe benefits (true value or cost of that person). For example, if your company provides engineering support with a staff costing $200,000 in annual salaries, add $50,000 (25 percent) before allocating the total cost to customers using the service.

The *A* stands for *assets*—equipment, buildings, trucks, other fixed values. For example, your company provides a free testing lab service to

IDEA   c o n t i n u e d

customers. You have to consider what the value is of all the lab equipment, facilities, and so forth, in defining the value of the service. Ask yourself: "What assets are involved in providing or realizing this benefit?" (In this example, the people who do the testing would also be added in as a resource.)

The *C* in IMPACT is for *capability,* an indicator of *how well or efficiently* something is being done. If you've been able to improve an operation, speed it up, and make it more productive (in other words, improve the efficiency of the people or equipment), you can measure it and convert it to a quantified benefit. For example, as a result of value-added training, you've improved productivity 10 percent. That 10 precent is your measure of capability (unless you can go further and convert the 10 percent to money saved).

The *T* means *time,* which is an important measure of efficiency in many operations. If you can help accounts collect their own accounts receivable faster, turn inventory over more quickly, speed up production, or provide more prompt delivery, you have added value; in such situations, time improvement or an account's increased ability to expedite tasks should be your means of measuring value added. For example, what's it worth to an account to get three-hour guaranteed service response time (without charge) when your competitors are all giving 24-hour service? How does your approach versus your competitors' approaches affect the account's downtime of equipment, work hours in which people stand idle, lost orders, production delays, and so on?

The six IMPACT resources are value indicators that work together to help you measure the value-added benefits you and your company provide. Estimating costs or benefit values enables you to provide values for a specific account. This is a creative process and requires thought, time, and logic. However, the result will be worth it and will enable you to optimize your value-added benefits and set the stage for powerful and memorable selling.

In summary, follow the steps below to quantify value-added benefits:

1. Recognize that all value-added benefits provide value to the customer, and that most values can be quantified.

2. When quantifying the value, the ideal method is to measure the benefit; but if this cannot be done, a fallback method is to quantify the cost of providing the service (what it costs your company to provide this benefit).

3. To quantify, use IMPACT to identify the interacting resources and then quantify the individual elements.

4. If more than one value-added benefit, service, or resource is involved, link them by adding or multiplying, as needed.

5. To maximize the value, project the benefits over the long term.

 C A S E   S T U D Y

QUANTIFYING VALUES

- An account manager sells paint-spraying equipment to manufacturers for finishing production-line products such as appliances, furniture, and small parts using various metals and woods. Because his company has recognized the thousands of applications and variables involved, it offers a testing laboratory as a free enhancement to its customers. The testing lab simulates the proposed application and materials and provides the customer with recommendations on paint type, coating thickness, drying time, and other pertinent specifications.

The account manager is preparing for a presentation to one of his important accounts, Major Appliance Corporation (MAC). His objective is to sell MAC on purchasing about $30,000 worth of additional paint-spraying equipment. However, he's about 10 percent higher than the main competitor and, while MAC prefers his equipment, it may question the price differential. Anticipating this, he's done some homework on this testing service and plans to bring up the value-added benefits during the presentation.

Research by the account manager has provided an estimate of annual costs for the company to provide this testing feature:

Space and equipment	$130,000
Personnel	$260,000
Operating expense and materials	$ 57,000

He's also learned that 400 tests were conducted last year for customers, including four for Major Appliance Corp.'s new product introductions and production changes.

The value the account manager uses is:

$$\frac{\$130,000 + \$260,000 + \$57,000}{400} = \$1,118 \text{ per test}$$

CASE STUDY continued

MAC's value = 4 × $1,118 = $4,472 per year, enough to differentiate the account manager's offer from the competition and make the sale!

- Standard Office Systems (SOS) is one account to which the sales rep has provided leasing services for the past three years. Now the sales rep is being challenged by a new competitor with slightly lower interest rates than she offers. SOS sells computers, copiers, and duplicating equipment and does most of its financing through the sales rep's company. Recognizing that she is going to have to confront the issue shortly, she's recalled some situations that give her leverage. Interest rates are pretty competitive, and basic services are similar. However, she has managed to provide SOS with a variety of *extra* services:

When her company turned down one of SOS's leases (XYZ Co.) because it was too risky, she immediately found SOS another finance company that would take the risk. This saved a $20,000 deal for SOS and earned it a 25 percent commission.

On one large deal for $100,000, the sales rep personally carried the paperwork through the maze, cutting the paperwork processing time from two weeks to two days. To accomplish this, she had to tie up two administrators for both days, plus devote a day of her own time. The sales rep estimated that these three days cost her company an extra $1,000.

On another $8,000 deal (which was eventually turned down), she anticipated a potential problem, checked with some banker contacts, and convinced SOS that its prospect was a bad risk. SOS's customer prospect eventually went into bankruptcy.

By using these value-added savings, the sales rep was able to protect her position with the account. Her value-added benefits totaled $136,000:

$$
\begin{array}{r}
\$\,25,000 \\
103,000 \\
\underline{8,000} \\
\end{array}
$$

Total: $136,000   (plus legal fees and interest)

To capitalize on these value-added services, the values themselves need to be very visible to the customer. "Visible" is not a strong enough word, perhaps, since many customers are smart enough to recognize the benefits on occasion. While being visible is part of the scheme, the benefits need to be memorable, dramatic, concrete, specific, and validated. After all, when translating value-added services into benefits, you are selling a concept. Concept-selling demands powerful benefits presented in a different way that positions you ahead of, and apart from, competitive companies. That's what differentiation is all about.

◇ Tactic 3: Sell Value-Added Benefits on Ongoing Sales Calls

If you've provided a significant value-added service to a customer, you should capitalize on it immediately, which may be your next sales call. As a sales professional, you probably don't need any coaching on how to present the significance of value-added benefits to your customers. However, some simple guidelines will no doubt reinforce your own tactics for delivering this message and help you achieve maximum impact and retention.

First, it's a good idea to use a bridging statement to lead into, identify, and illuminate the benefits. Value-added benefits are special and should be presented on their own stage, rather than merged with product benefits or presented casually. To set the stage, use a transition or bridge such as: "In addition to our normal service, we were pleased that we could allocate personnel for six store openings during the quarter. I estimate that this extra service saved you over $3,000 in actual costs and, equally important, added value to your openings."

Second, when dealing with numbers, always document your data to reinforce the specific and measurable values. There's nothing wrong with using a scratch pad to illustrate how you arrived at the values. Either show the customer your figures in a clear presentation put together in advance or dramatically re-create your estimates and calculations on the spot. If your numbers are visible, they will be remembered.

Immediate reinforcement is important and so is some type of "show and tell." Selling concepts, as in value-added services, demands a little showmanship to implant the idea and make it stick. In using "ongoing sales calls" as a tactic, you are using a set of building blocks to create a perception, so each block must be laid down carefully and cemented in place.

Third, if you are presenting to a new decision maker or a new account, be prepared to cite value-added success stories that you've generated for other accounts. Treat these experiences as "case studies" to differentiate your offering and buttress your presentation.

 I D E A

BE CREATIVE IN "SELLING" THE BENEFITS

There is no limit on creativity, as evidenced by the tactics being used by aggressive organizations to reinforce their value-added services, exemplified by the following:

- Vendor 1 issues a "no-charge" invoice each time it supplies a major value-added service to a customer. The invoice describes the service and indicates the value if a cost had been assigned to it. If appropriate, the salesperson will also explain and reinforce the value of the benefit to the customer when he or she delivers it.

- Vendor 2 routinely has its salespeople, who sell via formal proposal, itemize for the customer the value-added services it is supplying; they add a special section or paragraph. They also summarize the value of the benefits by adding a total dollar amount at the end.

◇ Tactic 4: Sell Value-Added Benefits at Business Reviews

If you are not using business reviews with major accounts as a sales tactic, you should. Many organizations (and salespeople) make this a major sales event for important accounts and use it as an opportunity to periodically review results and to discuss plans.

Most importantly, it's an opportunity to access the top guns of the account and bring in your own top-level management. It's a great showcase for summarizing and valuing the "free" services that you have provided during the year and to discuss those you plan to include in the future. What better way to bond with your customer!

Many of our clients track value-added services that they have generated in behalf of a specific account and itemize these services during their presentation. They obtain feedback from the customer that enables them to determine which services are needed for the future. Most importantly, they use this key presentation to build relationships and to subtly differentiate (and distance) themselves from the competition.

◇ Tactic 5: Sell Value-Added Services when Negotiating

While we treat negotiating as a major strategy (in a separate chapter), it deserves mention here as a powerful tactical means of capitalizing on value-added services. Negotiating is defined as "trading values," so value-added services (and their worth to the account) should logically become part of what's traded.

In the next chapter on the sales negotiating strategy, we'll take the values concept to another level, beyond just those provided by value-added services. However, it's important to recognize that negotiating

 **C A S E   S T U D Y**

NEGOTIATING WITH VALUE-ADDED SERVICES

A good example of how this technique works was demonstrated by a key account manager in the United Kingdom. As part of the work we were doing for this major grocery products firm, based in London, I accompanied this salesperson to a major negotiating session in Manchester. It's important to recognize that, unlike the United States, grocery vendors and customers in the United Kingdom sign annual contracts that "lock in" prices for the length of the contract. As a result, these commitments are seriously contested because even a 1 percent difference can result in huge savings for either party to the negotiation. In this instance, the buyer balked at signing the contract over a 1/2 percent difference until the account manager reviewed the value-added services his company had provided. He began talking first about a space-maximizer computer program the vendor had used (without cost to the customer) to increase profits by maximizing the most profitable products displayed. Within minutes, even before the account manager could move to a discussion of other value-added services, the buyer "surrendered" the 1/2 percent, giving into the powerful weight of the values provided.

(whether used as an on-the-spot tactic or employed as a long-term strategy) is more than just trading or "haggling"; it's a sophisticated process for convincing the adversary of the *value* of what he or she is giving up or getting. In this context, value-added services become a vital part of your negotiating tactic and long-term negotiating strategy.

◇ Tactic 6: Sell Value-Added Services in Competitive Situations

There is no more important scenario to differentiate yourself from the rest than in a competitive situation. Regardless of whether you are competing for a new account or trying to keep a competitor out, value-added services become a critical part of this tactic and overall strategy. In head-to-head competitive confrontations, the smart customer will consider what we call "the total offering" from each vendor. Traditionally, the total offering has been the product, the selling company and its capabilities, and support services. This competitive scenario becomes a significant opportunity to differentiate yourself, not only by comparing these three elements of the offering (product, company, service) in your tactical presentation, but also by adding a fourth benchmark, value-added services and the *values* to the customer.

In Exhibit 4.3 you'll see a tool that's used in competitive situations to plan presentations to differentiate the presenter from the competition via a feature-to-feature comparison. Note the large section (circled) for value-added services. In our experience, the value-added services section usually makes the difference in capturing the business. Your competitor can have his own value-added services but may not capitalize on them or know-how to use this strategy. That's where your skills and knowledge come into play to gain a competitive edge.

In the final analysis, every buyer is a value buyer at heart. While strong relationships, actual service, good products, vendor reliability, and image are important, it's the total value that provides the differentiation between you and your competitor. Chances are that your competitor has not considered this powerful advantage or taken the time to identify specific services, to value them, and to use them in the sales process. In short, the introduction and use of value-added services are your competitive edge, when you apply the strategy outlined herein.

Let's end this chapter with a review of the critical steps needed to optimize this strategy and the results it will generate. Most importantly,

E X H I B I T   4 . 3

Inventory of Value-Added Services

TOTAL OFFERING PORTFOLIO (TOP)

Competitor: _____ACME_____

FEATURE CHECKLIST	ADVANTAGE High	Med.	Low	None	ADVANTAGE DIFFERENTIATION
[√] P/S 1 ALPHA				X	
[√] P/S 2 BETA			X		
[√] P/S 4 GAMMA		X			
[ ] P/S 5					
[ ] P/S 6					
[ ] P/S 5					
[ ] P/S 6					
[ ] Advertising/ merchandising					
[√] Cost/profit			X		
[√] Credit				X	
[√] Delivery		X			
[ ] Focus/experience					
[ ] Growth/new products					
[ ] Location/proximity					
[ ] Packaging					
[√] Performance/results		X			
[ ] Pull-through					
[ ] Market share					
[ ] Relationship					
[ ] Reputation/image					
[ ] Research/engineering					
[√] Service/response time	X				
[ ] Size/resources					
[√] Systems fit			X		
[ ] Technical support					
[√] Value-added services					
[√] *Training*	X				No value-added
[√] *Just-in-time del.*	X				For ACME!!
[√] *Free survey*	X				
[ ]					
[ ]					

 **RED FLAG**

DON'T TAKE SHORTCUTS

If you've read this far, and sense that this strategy will work for you, don't take a shortcut. A shortcut is perceiving this as a piecemeal tactic (rather than a strategy), not doing your homework on determining values, and failing to "sell" this concept at *every* opportunity.

in selling concepts, you must sell the concept at every level and at every opportunity. The objective of this strategy is to create a *total* perception at the account. "Winning" a negotiation or competitive situation, or even overcoming an objection with value-added services, is tactical. The big win will come as a result of many actions and tactics wrapped in a cohesive plan of attack—a strategy.

To implement the strategy effectively:

1. Take an inventory of value-added services that you can provide and those supplied to customers.

2. Value the most important services you provide (greatest value or those used most frequently) and be prepared to document them in terms of dollar benefits.

3. Use the tactics on ongoing sales calls, during business reviews, in negotiations, and competitive situations.

The value-added concept may sound simplistic, but it's difficult to implement as a strategy without a plan, creativity, and perseverance. However, if done properly, the results over time will be significant and will dramatically enhance your regular sales efforts and enable you to differentiate yourself from the competition. In this manner, both you and the customer benefit from the values.

5

C H A P T E R

Sales Negotiating Strategy

NEGOTIATING WITH CUSTOMERS IS UNIQUE!

As a professional salesperson, you should recognize that sales negotiating is quite different from other types of negotiating scenarios. Historically, negotiating has probably been evolving since medieval times. In more recent decades, negotiation has been used to settle disputes, end wars, resolve labor–management strife, dissolve marriages, and so on.

While much of the strategy and various skills can be transferred to the sales arena, there are some major cautions. The major difference between sales negotiating and other types of negotiations is the *customer*. More importantly, it's the preservation of the customer through the negotiating process that is really key.

Most nonsales negotiating occurs between adversaries. *Adversary,* as you know, is a euphemism for opponent or enemy. The word *adversary* will seldom be confused with *customer*. The first major difference, then, is the fact that you have to be collaborative when negotiating, and the end result should be win–win for both of you.

Another difference is that sales negotiating is not a one-time event. There may be many opportunities to use this strategy with the same (and different) customers. In fact, the nature of sales negotiating may be ongoing; the same issues are negotiated over many calls, or you may have customers who try to negotiate something on *every* call! At times, it's difficult to tell when selling ends and negotiating begins, or vice versa. The two skills often flow together as one.

One similarity between sales and nonsales negotiating relates to the topic of power. As we move into this chapter, we'll cover the issue of power and who has the power going into a negotiation. For most nonsales negotiations, the power is generally balanced before negotiating starts. After all, why would the participants be negotiating if it weren't? You may be thinking your customers have the power. So why negotiate? Not so. You'll find that it works both ways, and that one of your objectives in negotiating with customers is to make sure the power is balanced. It's all part of the strategy.

As a result, the sales negotiation is truly different from other types of negotiating. If further belief is required, let's eliminate the casual customer confrontations or "handling an objection"—that's not what the sales negotiating strategy is all about. The sales negotiation strategy can be proactive, initiated by the salesperson, to get the business; it can be defensive also, but it's never done by the pros "on the spot." That's too tactical! Sales negotiating strategy, as you will see, is a series of actions requiring strategy (planning) and tactics, and an important negotiation can take weeks or months to accomplish. Some customers try to negotiate on almost every call and, in doing so, provide a specific meaning to the word *ongoing.*

SALES NEGOTIATING STRATEGY DEFINED

Sales negotiating strategy, a process between the customer and the vendor, is geared to exchange values. It can be triggered by either party and should be win–win. In other words, it needs to be collaborative overall (but not exclusively), and both you and the customer need to have an agreement that is fair. Both parties need to win. Sales negotiations are often triggered by value differences or conflicts over perceived value that affect mutual interests. Because of the important values, and the need to carefully plan, a true sales negotiation should not surface suddenly on a sales call. If the issue can be handled on the spot, it simply is not strategic sales negotiating; it's tactical "handling of sales resistance." Additionally, if the customer introduces a negotiating possibility for anything of significant value, you'd be wise to tactfully postpone the negotiation until you can develop your strategy.

The bottom line in terms of sales negotiating strategy is that you are trading with the customer and dealing with a wider range of issues than price alone. The objective in this kind of sales negotiating is to get equal value for everything you give up. However, unlike wrestling with a dealer at a flea market, where you haggle over price, price may not even be an issue. The win–win strategic negotiation is characterized by a need to maintain the sales process and the harmony of the relationship while values are being exchanged.

 ## CASE STUDY

PHARMACEUTICAL ACCOUNT MANAGER NEGOTIATES WITH HMO

In the dynamic 1990s, managed health care was one significant change that everyone adapted to. At the controls, we now have a managed health maintenance organization (HMO) that has taken away the brand decision power from the physician. Consequently, most major drugs must be approved contractually by the HMO before the affiliated physicians can prescribe them.

In pursuit of a contract for a "hot" new drug, Brand A, Kent Harris spent many calls setting the stage for what he considered a series of negotiations to gain approval with the formulary committee of the HMO. He knew that cost would certainly be an issue, but not the only one. His pharmaceutical company had the ability, largely through its national sales team, to quickly educate the dermatologists and promote the drug at the patient level. He also recognized the need to gain a contract for a minor product of his, Drug B, so he decided to include both drugs when the negotiations began. Over a series of weeks, he and other pharmaceutical executives from his company worked on many issues, but always with one concept in mind: If we have to trade, let's get equal value in return. For example, to protect what they felt was the best selling price (to the HMO), they offered to provide extra "value" by developing both a newsletter and an educational video for the physician population. When they presented the values of what they were offering, it became apparent to the HMO that these value-added services certainly matched the additional profits derived from a "price concession." Finally, at the appropriate time, when a tentative agreement had been reached for all the issues regarding Drug A, the concept of Drug B (an "older" drug prescribed by nephrologists) was introduced. Since Drug B was to replace a

CASE STUDY continued

competitive drug on the HMO's formulary, Kent's team offered a better unit price than the competitor, backing up the offer with a commitment to handle the total cost of physician conversion for both drugs. Deploying their sales force to call on all dermatologists and nephrologists in the HMO system, they would help each doctor during the transition and promote doctor awareness of prescribing conditions, dosing, patient costs, and side effects. The commitment was finally made for both drugs, and a win–win arrangement for both parties was agreed. Did each party achieve everything it wanted? Not exactly! However, the contracts provided a negotiating win–win.

While this is a short synopsis of a reasonably long and perhaps complicated sales negotiation, one with less at stake may have similar parameters and timeliness. The key to the success was strategy, planning, and execution, coupled with collaborative give-and-take throughout.

THE SALES NEGOTIATION STRATEGIC MODEL OVERVIEW

Sales negotiating has a shorter implementation cycle than more complex strategies, but the process still needs a track to run on. In brief, there are three major, defined steps: (1) analyze the situation, (2) plan the negotiation, and (3) negotiate. (See Exhibit 5.1.)

Analyze the situation, the first step, is an assessment tactic, and while some of the input may evolve from sales calls, it's more a question of thinking and focus. This step enables you to assess four critical and interacting checkpoints before deciding if this is the right time or right issue to negotiate:

1. Look at the *power* status between you and the customer. Is it reasonably balanced?
2. Assess the customer's *positions.* Where is he or she "at" on specific issues? What's the *interest* behind each position?
3. Ask yourself if the *competition* is in the picture, and how strong a factor it will be.
4. Consider if this is an *opportunity* to negotiate. If so, what are the risks?

If you take this step carefully, you will know whether to negotiate or not, to trigger it yourself, or to wait for the customer to take the initiative.

EXHIBIT 5.1

Strategic Sales Negotiating Model

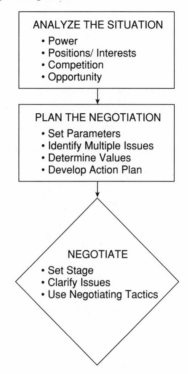

Assuming you decide to proceed, the next step, *plan the negotia-tion,* becomes your platform for successful strategizing. In this step you do the following:

- *Set parameters.* These are your limits—the minimum and the maximum you can offer.
- *Identify multiple issues.* There's nothing more deadly than trying to negotiate a single issue such as price; if you do, you have little to trade or to ask for in return.
- *Determine values.* Yes, we're back to values. Everything has a value and you need to know rough values if you're going to trade successfully. How else will you know what you're negotiating with or asking for in return?
- *Develop an action plan.* The last part of this step involves putting your game plan together in a sequence, so you can be prepared for the give-and-take of negotiation. Like an effective

sales call, a good negotiating session (or sessions) can be planned, without putting on a "straitjacket"; a flexible plan will provide a track to run on, prepare you for surprises, and arm you with contingencies.

The third step in the model, *negotiate,* can involve one or many sessions (sales calls). To some degree it's free form, due to the nature of the negotiation, which is 100 percent tactical. While no one can totally anticipate the customer's reactions to each exchange, it's pertinent to cover these tactics:

- *Set the stage.* This ensures that all parties understand the nature and objectives of the meeting.
- *Clarify issues as you go along.* This takes skill, although good salespeople do it instinctively, to make sure that there is complete understanding and communication throughout the process.
- *Use negotiating tactics.* While there are hundreds of so-called negotiating tactics—from dealing with terrorists to unions to attorneys and to every conceivable business situation—there are only a few that are important (and work) in the sales/customer scenario. The tactics we'll cover don't fall into the "magic formula" category; like most tactics they are professional and are designed to encourage and maintain a collaborative climate between the seller and the buyer.

The balance of this chapter will focus on these tactics for implementing strategic sales negotiating.

☐ Tactic 1: Analyze the Situation

Analyzing the account situation is something most salespeople do well, since they have general access to their best customers and frequently visit their premises and facilities. However, they are usually analyzing the account for opportunities to build relationships, find new applications, identify needs, learn the customer's business, solve problems. When anticipating or starting a negotiation, some of these needs change, and others require a different focus. At least four interacting indicators should be examined before deciding if negotiation is the best strategy to employ and/or what's the best approach to take in implementing it.

⚑ RED FLAG

DON'T LOSE SIGHT OF YOUR OBJECTIVES

It's imperative to keep twin objectives in your head (and heart) and never lose sight of them. While an obvious goal of the sales negotiating strategy is to build your business with the customer, there are two critical objectives you should constantly focus on. One objective is that the ideal customer negotiation (if there is an ideal!) should be win–win. In other words, you and the customer must feel that you both had gains and that the negotiation was conducted in a collaborative manner. While this may seem like a "blinding glimpse of the obvious," you should recognize the underlying tension and manage it. The second red flag, and one that drives the strategy, is the need to recognize values and, within reason, trade value for value. For example, if you have to give up something, you should get reasonable value for it in return. Likewise, if you need something of value from the customer, be prepared to trade equal value. These objectives form the basis for any effective and winning negotiation between you and the customer.

Ramp Up the Power (On Both Sides!)

One indicator that should be carefully scrutinized is the power—who has it? While most salespeople think the customer *always* has the power (and plenty of it), that's a fallacy. While the power can be heavy on the customer's end, it can also be weighted toward the seller. For example, suppose you're dealing with a good account, whose priorities have changed suddenly, and it requires expedited delivery of significant orders from your company. Who has the power? In this situation, if the delivery can be expedited, the seller has the power. However, you can't abuse the situation and ask for more (in return) than expediting the delivery is worth.

The main idea in examining the power *before* entering a specific situation is to make sure the power is reasonably balanced on both sides. While the customer has the power to provide business, sign orders, make demands, and so on, there are many power issues in your favor, and the prudent customer will not risk losing them. After all, you provide quality products and services, have learned the customer's business, provide value-added services, have developed relationships, and probably have an edge over the competition. One of your power pluses, it is hoped, is your superior ability in executing a sales negotiating strategy. Don't ever sell your power short!

This power assessment serves as a reality check:

- If you have an excess of power, be careful and don't abuse it during the negotiation. You may win the battle but shoot yourself in the foot on a long-term basis by not orchestrating a win–win solution or by allowing stress to neutralize relationships.
- If the customer has an excess of power, this situation may be the one you should decline or tactfully avoid entering into.

Power is a state of mind, and by assessing the power balance each time you'll probably find that you have more power than you thought!

What's the Interest behind Each Position?

Another element that needs to be carefully assessed or analyzed is the customer's position and interest. In simple terms, a position is what the customer wants (or will ask for). You will often know some of his or her positions before the negotiation. Positions are difficult to change unless you can pinpoint the interest behind the position; in other words, it's necessary to probe into what's causing the customer to take the position. A customer who seeks a 10 percent discount on a large order is taking a position. If you take this at face value, you can negotiate only this position. However, when you probe the interest (behind the position) you may uncover a number of interests that can be more successfully negotiated, and you can find better ways to handle it. In terms of this hypothetical customer's 10 percent discount position, the interest could be a budget cut, need for better terms, a concern about getting more value from purchases, an ego demand on the customer's part, a desire to look good by saving money, and so on. It should be obvious that the latter "interests" are easier to negotiate than a concrete demand for a 10 percent discount. Finding the interest(s) opens up many additional opportunities for creative solutions and trades.

Once you know the position, how do you find the interest? You simply use your tactical selling skills. By probing for the reasons behind the position, you may uncover some clues to the request; this is one way to effectively capitalize on relationships before you find

 **C A S E   S T U D Y**

FINDING THE INTEREST BEHIND THE POSITION

Recently, Porter Henry & Co. was involved in serious negotiations with a new client, a major supplier of paint and spraying equipment, to outsource its sales training for distributors. We'll call them Client A.

While many of the issues were successfully negotiated over a series of meetings, one position issue kept surfacing. Client A was aware that we were working with one of its competitors (Client B) and felt (strongly, it seemed) that this would be a negative factor; in other words, Client A wanted an exclusive arrangement, so the apparent options seemed to be (1) terminate our relationship with Client B, or (2) wait until Client B's current contract was completed and then sign on with new Client A. Neither of these options were acceptable to us. In our strategy meetings, we felt that the reason for this request was confidentiality, but we agreed to probe this issue and find out what the interest really was.

Within minutes of asking a few key questions, we had the interest on the table and a contract in our hands. Client A simply envisioned our relationship (alliance) as a major and unique strategy that it planned to use to set up a "Distributor University," with the intention of marketing this as a value-added service to its distributors. When we explained that Client B was a transactional client (we did piecemeal projects from time to time), that paint was a minor product line, and that it was marketed through different channels, the issue disappeared. All we had to do was commit to providing Client A with an exclusive contract in its industry for this type of outsourced program, and we were off and running. This issue had come up three to four times in different ways in various negotiations, but only until it became a major issue (after other issues had been negotiated) did we have enough sense to ask why. To paraphrase the axiom about the shoemaker's children going barefoot: "Sometimes the consultant's children don't practice what they preach."

---

yourself in a negotiating session. If you can't uncover the interest before negotiation, you can certainly ask during negotiating. However, you lose the advantage of knowing in advance (and being able to plan your strategy). Better to plan and to ask your questions while in the analysis step.

E X H I B I T   5 . 2

Decision Matrix for Negotiating

POWER Customer: H M L	My company: H M L
POSITIONS:	INTERESTS (*Why* the position?):
1. _____	1. _____
2. _____	2. _____
COMPETITION: H M L NA	
Strengths:	Weaknesses:
1. _____	1. _____
2. _____	2. _____

Check Out the Competition

Another indicator that needs to be assessed in this first step is the competition. Competition may not be a factor, and in most sales negotiations it should not be. The general rule for negotiation is that "if the customer negotiates, he has made a mental decision to purchase and is merely seeking a better deal." That's pretty sound, but it's very precarious if he's negotiating with your competition simultaneously or using them for leverage. In either case, your analysis should be applied to the situation if a competitor lurks in the wings; if so, do a quick feature/benefit analysis to compare your strengths and weaknesses with the competition's. You can thus arm yourself with appropriate offers to offset the competitive issues, if they surface.

Go or No-Go Decision?

The final indicator for you to ponder: Is this a productive opportunity to negotiate with the customer? This is the bottom line for you, and the platform for your strategy. In brief, you need to weigh the risks and determine if you should proceed (perhaps initiate the negotiation yourself) or dodge it, assuming the customer is pressing you for a negotiating solution. One method for deciding is to use a simple decision matrix that helps you objectively weigh the factors, as in Exhibit 5.2.

I D E A

KNOW WHEN TO INITIATE THE NEGOTIATION

Assuming that most of the assessments indicate a "go," it's still necessary to determine if you should initiate the negotiation or leave it up to the customer to be proactive. If you've gone this far in assessing the situation, the customer has indicated (via a problem, complaint, objection, or direct request) that she's seeking "extra value" or concessions, so you may not have any choice but to mentally begin the process. On the other hand, the situation may not be that clear-cut, either because the customer hasn't communicated the situation or need clearly, or because she doesn't see negotiating as a solution.

Here are some simple guidelines for entering into or initiating the negotiation, after you've done your homework (above) and feel that the risk is low. Begin to negotiate when:

1. The customer has made strong signals or demands, and you are prepared to provide some concessions.

2. The customer is stalling over a major issue (on initial sale or ongoing problem), and you suspect you will have to eventually provide some concessions.

3. In both situations 1 and 2, you have some values or concessions that you would like *in return.*

In short, the object of the decision matrix is to rank your power and that of the customer's as high (H), medium (M), or low (L) for this possible negotiation. Beware if either you or the customer are at opposite poles (high or low).

If you can't identify at least one (and probably two) positions that the customer will take, you are not ready to negotiate. The solution is to do more tactful probing so you can arm yourself. You may or may not be able to surface the interest in this step, but that's OK. This gap (empty space under "Interests") will reinforce the need to locate the interest(s) later in your planning and actual negotiating.

Finally, you quickly assess if competition is a factor (high, medium, low, or not applicable). If it is high or medium, then it would be a good idea to examine both strengths and weaknesses of the competition's offering as compared to the strengths and weaknesses of yours.

If all conditions are met, it's academic who initiates the negotiation. Go for it! But first go to the next step to make sure you have a trading situation and have completed a balanced action plan.

☐ Tactic 2: Plan the Negotiation

Planning is essential, due to the unknown demands and responses, the give-and-take of negotiating. Even though there's no such thing as a perfect tactical plan for negotiating, a good plan will certainly help. It will eliminate surprises, enable you to anticipate customer moves, and arm you with contingencies. The four interacting components of a useful negotiating plan—set parameters, identify multiple issues, determine values, and develop action plan–are explained in the upcoming pages.

Set Parameters

- What is the *minimum* that I will offer this customer?
- What is the *maximum* that I can offer this customer?

While the questions are simple, the answers are more complex. And rightfully so. The parameters, or questions, define your playing field and are the boundaries for executing your strategy. They initiate the thought process, forcing you to gauge what the customer wants and to dig deep into your own inventory (what you can trade) to assess what you can give. The parameters become twin goalposts that force you to come up with a supporting game plan—nothing more or less. They also become a silent reminder (and commitment to yourself) that you will not, and should not, exceed them.

Here's a final word about parameters. We're not talking about giving the store away or discounting. What you "give" may be extra service, faster delivery, special packaging, better credit terms, "free" goods, added features, technical help, guarantees of performance. Yes, discounts, lower costs, and refunds may be part of it, but they are not necessarily the only values involved. Everything has value, particularly when negotiating. More about the specific values later.

Identify Multiple Issues

A second part of your negotiating game plan is identifying multiple negotiating issues.

A negotiable issue is a component of your total offering (products, services, delivery, pricing, credit terms, etc.), and in negotiating this becomes the vehicle you use for trading. It's what you and the customer employ to resolve differences. An issue can be many things: product features, benefits, price, delivery, service, advertising, terms, and so on. Negotiable issues, in essence, *are what you want and what the customer wants,* and therefore issues can be related to any aspect of your total product/service offering.

There are many reasons for broadening negotiations by introducing multiple issues:

- Since many negotiations are triggered by customers and usually conducted on their premises, the customer may have an unfair advantage. Introducing your issues offsets this advantage.
- Broadening the negotiation also eliminates piecemeal or single-issue negotiating that can be one-sided. For example, simply dealing with price leaves you with little to trade.
- Introducing your issues enables you to balance trading, accomplish related sales objectives, and implement win–win negotiating.

To broaden the negotiation, you start by taking inventory of all the issues—what you want and what the customer wants. This enables you to look for possible trades and will reinforce the point that negotiation involves issues from both sides, not just the customer's. Later, when we get to specific negotiation tactics, you'll see the importance of having a broad menu of issues so you can balance customer requests for demands with issues that you want.

Determine Values

A third and related element of your game plan is the need to determine (and use) values for what you plan to trade. How else can you get value for what you have to offer (give up)? Negotiating is often painful for inexperienced sales negotiators. They believe they are at a disadvantage with the customer and may wind up with their backs against the wall. This is not so, if you develop a passion for asking for something of equal value in return. It's a mind-set that successful negotiators adopt, and it's an issue about which they are adamant when embroiled in the heat of trading. Not only do you get something of equal value if the trade works, but you also gain added power by asking for something in return for a concession. Such trading savvy puts the customer on the defensive and provides a monitor of how much he or she will demand, and how frequently such demands may occur.

For example, if customer X asks for a 2 percent discount (which you can accommodate), simply come back with: "We might be able to do that, but I would need a commitment from you for an extra $250,000 of volume this year." The assumption in this illustration is that the 2 percent discount has about the same value as the extra sales volume. Your request for additional business will cause the customer to pause and think. In the process, the customer loses some momentum and must consider backing off on the request or moving forward with a "trade."

How do you determine the values? Once you have the multiple issues identified for both sides, you can estimate the cost of each side's request by using the same method suggested in Chapter 4. If desired, you can use the IMPACT formula described in Chapter 4 to identify the values for each issue on both your side and the customer's. However, you don't have to be very precise when determining a value; you only need an estimate. This knowledge will not only reinforce your power and control the trading, but it will also arm you in the event the customer questions or challenges your rationale. It's important to recognize that, when you are in the tactical or negotiating stage of this strategy, you are being challenged to think on your feet. If you have estimated your values ahead of time, you can focus on sales and negotiating tactics. This underlines the value of having a strategy, which requires planning.

A few years ago we were negotiating with a video producer for a major video that was being integrated into a series of proprietary strategic sales programs we were developing. In this situation, I was the customer. Once we had arrived at price or budget, I wanted to negotiate favorable terms, based on future sales of these four new products. Since it was impossible to determine a percentage (such as a 10 percent royalty) of sales over time, I had prepared a projection of our sales for each of the four products, so it was relatively easy to anticipate the values and how long it would take to reach them. The deal was accomplished, but only because the estimated values had been determined ahead of time.

Develop Action Plan

The fourth step in planning the negotiation is developing a tight action plan to help structure the "selling" tactics. Since the actual negotiation is often free form and reactional, you need a structure to help you manage the process and keep you on track. It's guaranteed that your customer, while having a set of demands and positions, will not have a game plan that rivals yours. If you feel that your customer has more power going

I D E A

PLAN MULTIPLE ISSUES AND VALUES TOGETHER

Since the issues on both sides (yours and the account's) are relative to each other, it's a good idea to merge both concepts into one clear picture.

In Exhibit 5.3 you'll get a rough idea of how the values might be balanced to achieve a win for both parties. In this exhibit, the worksheet values will never totally balance, but by having a measure of what the values are, (1) you will know where you are going and (2) if needed during the negotiation, you can clarify a situation by sharing the values with the customer.

E X H I B I T   5.3

Negotiable Issues and Values

Account's Issues	Value	Our Issues	Value
30 day trial	Peace of mind; no dollar value, but could cost them in terms of delays	Want new product approval as soon as possible	Could save customer about $50,000 a year
		Can offer up to 5% discount on truckloads	$17,000
Extra help/training for installation	About $1,000 expense to us	Permission to use account as reference	Big help to us
10% discount on truckload shipments	Estimated annual savings: $34,000	Protect existing share of business plus new product addition	$340,000 a year

into a negotiation, a tight game plan on your end will do wonders to enhance your power (and provide a level playing field). Like any good plan, it should be flexible; in addition, it should contain goals to keep you on track, a possible scenario for making trades, and a workable sequence. You don't want to make the action plan so tight that you put yourself in a straitjacket, but you do need a road map of how to get to win–win through balanced trading. In Exhibit 5.4 you'll see a worksheet plan, including parameters (your goal lines) and a sequence of tradable options or issues, including values. In this projected scenario, the sales negotiator has even included possible negotiating tactics to use to present or frame each trade. (We'll discuss specific negotiating tactics in the next step.)

Exhibit 5.4 is not a highly structured plan nor should you create one. Every negotiation is filled with bumps and detours. However, by having done a "dry run" like this, you'll have an assortment of moves that you can make, and you'll have a logical track to run on. Without it, you'll be dealing from instinct and reaction alone—a dangerous route for a salesperson to take with a customer. Your entire sales negotiating strategy is crystallized in one or more face-to-face negotiations; therefore, a thoughtful, but flexible, plan will provide you with more options and contingencies and enable you to assess your progress as you work through this dynamic situation.

◇ Tactic 3: Negotiate

By now, you should have the idea that strategic sales negotiating is *not* a casual or piecemeal event—it takes big-time preparation. To negotiate successfully with customers, you have to earn the right through preparation, anticipation, and strategizing! As we move into the portion requiring real skill—the actual negotiation—a variety of skills and tactics come into play. The actual negotiating part of the overall strategy is dynamic and can be stressful. The better prepared you are, with game plans and moves, the more collaborative and productive will be the return.

Set the Stage

The first skill is setting the stage for the negotiation. It's not a difficult skill to master, but it is very important. If you've done this effectively, it will be clear to both you and the customer that you are negotiating. Like a selling situation, in which you plan an opener to set the stage for a sales call, you need a similar lead-in to set the stage for negotiation. There should be no doubt as to your objectives and intent, if the stage is set properly. An effective negotiating lead-in to set the stage should be no more than a sentence or two covering:

EXHIBIT 5.4

IV. PREPARING TO PRESENT OPTIONS AND OBTAIN FEEDBACK

Parameters:

What's the minimum I can offer (and keep the account happy)?

3% discount on combined product truckloads

Visit satisfied customer

What's the maximum I can offer (and keep us happy)?

5% discount on combined product truckloads

Two-week trial period

Present a Sequenced Offer of Tradable Options		
What I will offer to account	What I will ask for from account	Tactics
3% discount	*Try to get them to visit a satisfied customer instead of trial*	*Trade-off*
Values: $150	*Will save $300+*	
4% discount and one-week trial with personal follow-up	*Waive extra help training during implementation*	*Trade-off*
Values: $200	*$200 – $250*	
4.75% discount and two-week trial	*Permission to use account for future third-party references*	*Trial Balloon Reinforcements (Get boss on phone)*
Values: $240	*?*	
Values: $		
5% discount and two-week trial	*Immediate order approved upon successful completion of trail*	*Jujitsu* *Forbearance*
Values: $250		

- Your objectives for this session (to negotiate, clarify, or resolve a specific issue or problem).
- A collaboration on a win–win solution—one that both parties can be comfortable with.
- A brief update on how this issue surfaced, and what has transpired to date, including additional research you may have done, or discussions with other decision makers.
- Any other guidelines that might be helpful—timeliness, handling interruptions.

This will clear the air and establish a fair and collaborative climate. Unlike combative negotiations, such as those that often occur in real estate, union–management, legal, marital, and other adversarial situations, both parties need to be focused on making this a fair and timely "discussion." Setting the stage properly will usually do the trick and may be as simple as this:

> Bob, I know you have some concerns about budget and service, so we've agreed today to deal with these issues, as well as some requests from our end. I trust that, by the end of this session, we'll both agree that we've achieved our objectives through give-and-take on the important issues. I'm confident that in the next few hours we can work out a win–win solution.

Clarify Issues

The next component of the negotiating tactic is making sure you clarify issues. This is a difficult skill or tactic to describe, but, were it omitted, this book would be doing the sales negotiator a disservice. Clarifying issues is something you do throughout the negotiation, and you do it in many ways. For example, you can clarify an issue when it is introduced by you or the customer defining specifically what's being offered or asked for. You can also clarify an issue after it's been proposed, either by summarizing where you are or asking for feedback. The following are examples of questions that would elicit the kind of information you would want. "How does this sound?" "Are you comfortable with this exchange?" "Up until this point, we've agreed to modify the vents on our equipment, along with one of the drives. You're willing to increase your order to 125 units to help us offset the extra cost. Is that agreeable so far?"

The negotiating tactics that are covered next are basically communication devices, which help clarify the issues as they present, offset, or modify various offerings and trades. Clarification may also involve asking a decision maker why he is taking a specific position (in other words, asking for the interest behind the position). As you probably realize, clarifying issues is simply being very specific, tactful, communicating effectively, and providing much feedback to ensure understanding. Because of the pace and dynamics of negotiating and due to the constant flow of information, it's critical to make sure of complete understanding on both sides at every step. In selling, the same importance exists. In pure selling, if you omit a benefit or major point or the customer does not completely understand, you can always backtrack or catch up on the next call. Not so, with negotiating! This is a progressive action with few opportunities to go back. The nature of the process is to keep trading and building on past moves, so you need to know exactly where you have been, and so does the customer.

Use Negotiating Tactics

Negotiating tactics are the tools you use to present options and defend your positions, to clarify, or to establish a better negotiating framework. Each tactic has its own objective, since most are used differently and under various circumstances to position you for collaborative trading. Some are used to persuade, others help get the customer focused, and some are effective communication devices that provide a safety net against miscommunication for both sides.

 **RED FLAG**

BEWARE OF CHARLATANS AND TRICKY TACTICS

Negotiating tactics come in all shapes and sizes, and if your in-box looks like mine, you probably have received a ton of material on topics such as "Power Negotiating Made Easy," "The Secrets of the World's Great Negotiators," or "Tactics I Used to Negotiate 50 Million Dollars." Beware of instant fixes and miracle tactics such as "The Red Herring," "The Vise," or other cosmetic ploys that enable you to "destroy the guy across the table." These gambits may work in another world, but there's no room in a professional sales environment for manipulation and trickery. The key words, as this chapter emphasizes, are collaborative and win–win. Following are a number of tactics that successful salespeople use to negotiate with customers. You have to understand the concept or use of each, determine if it fits your style and customer base, and use each at the appropriate time. No quick fixes, and that's a promise! Like any skill, the menu of tactics below must be mastered through practice. The only promise that comes on the "wrapper" is that they are professional and work effectively under the right conditions.

NEGOTIATING TACTICS THAT WORK

Negotiating tactics are used to position your offer or solicit a trade in return. As you read about the following tactics, keep in mind that they are simply communication devices—not magic formulas for hypnotizing your accounts. They are tools to help you frame your offer and to convince (as in selling) the customer that the logic of your offer is valid. Like any tactic, they require skill and practice. You will never use all of them in a single negotiation, and chances are that you will never use all of them in a lifetime of sales negotiating. Think of these tactics as a toolbox or library that you can draw from to enhance your strategy as you focus on the face-to-face negotiation. These tactics will help you shape your offers and find out what the other person wants (and why).

Trade-off Tactic

Of all the sales negotiating tactics, the *trade-off* is used most often. Trading is the "heart and soul" of negotiating, and, for that reason, it may be the most important tactic. Trade-off basically means making an offer (issue) in return for the customer's concession(s). It's a technique of give-and-take, voluntarily substituting and bargaining one issue for another.

Here are some critical trade-off guidelines you should use in your negotiating sessions:

- Avoid making concessions too early in the negotiation. When you begin too early, it gives the customer the impression that you will "give" and keep giving, and that will put you under pressure.
- Concede slowly when making trades. The reason is the same as above; conceding too quickly puts you in a weak position and gives the customer a psychological advantage.
- Concede in progressively diminishing increments. This is important because it enables you to move slowly in successively smaller steps toward a mutually satisfying position or agreement. For example, if you have to concede a discount of 2 percent on your first offer, next you could possibly go to 3 percent, and then to 3 1/2 percent, etc.
- Concede in small increments; beware of big jumps that will encourage the customer to make big requests.

- Don't be the first to make a *major* concession, since this again gives the customer a psychological advantage. On the other hand, you gain an advantage by being the first to make a *minor* concession—this indicates a positive, flexible attitude, a willingness to bend and work with the account.
- Finally, don't concede too much as a deadline approaches. Having parameters in mind will protect you from being pressured by deadlines—artificial or real. You may also wish to use the subtactic of negotiating the deadline itself, and postpone or delay it.

Trial-Balloon Tactic

Trial balloon is a method of presenting the customer with options by prefacing your offer with the words "what if . . . ?" You don't commit yourself, but you bring the item up for discussion and, at the same time, give the customer the first right of refusal. This tactic enables you to constantly test the account, to assess and read interests and positions each time you put up a trial balloon. Obviously, you have to listen to responses and use your other sales skills to evaluate each response. To employ this tactic effectively, avoid using it too often in a specific negotiation, and alternate your "what if . . . ?" phrases with words like: "Suppose I could . . ." or "I'm not sure that it can be done, but how would you react if we could . . . ?"

An account manager for a major beer distributor supplies a classic example of the trial-balloon tactic. He had been struggling for some time with one of his large package store accounts to set up major displays, but the customer insisted it couldn't be done during high-traffic hours. Unfortunately, the store was scheduled for delivery at the height of its rush period. Finally, using the trial-balloon tactic, he said, "What if I can get our delivery routing changed to . . . ?" When the customer said yes, the account manager convinced the routing manager to find a suitable window for delivery and got his permanent display space.

Apparent Withdrawal Tactic

Apparent withdrawal implies you might withdraw, or it may indicate you are planning another move. The rationale is that you hope the customer will not press for further concessions in the face of your apparent with-drawal. This is largely a defensive maneuver, brought into play when you are losing ground or feeling pressure.

The skill in using this tactic is knowing both *when* and *how* to use it. You have to be subtle and imply that you may have to withdraw or postpone the negotiation. Your intent is not actually to withdraw, of course, but to tactfully let the account know the withdrawal or postpone-ment is a possibility unless the discussion changes direction.

However, if you do withdraw (or more likely postpone the negotia-tion) the time-out enables you to reconnoiter. During the withdrawal or postponement, you can buy strategizing time or use the delay to get help from others in your organization.

Feinting/Diverting Tactic

Feinting/diverting is designed to distract or lead the customer away from the main issues. It requires that you stress unimportant or lesser points. You make small concessions seem very important and cause him or her to work very hard for small gains. Ultimately, when you get to the impor-tant issues, you will have an advantage, since it will appear to the cus-tomer that you've already conceded on a number of "important" issues.

In practice, you might offer flexible terms (even if the customer doesn't need them) or provide additional service. In offering these con-cessions, you simultaneously expedite the presentation of a major de-mand by the customer, such as a heavy discount or addition of a major component without charge. In any case, your prior concessions will dis-courage or deter further requests; if they are introduced in the process anyway, your previous offers help offset the critical issue.

Fait Accompli Tactic

Fait accompli is French for "deed accomplished" and is presumably irre-versible. It is an assumptive tactic presenting the customer with a com-pleted action indicating the offer has already been implemented. Ways of using this tactic range from advising the customer that you have already scheduled his or her pickup beginning next week to informing the cus-tomer that the papers have already been processed and mailed.

This tactic should be used carefully and in a situation where the cus-tomer is hesitating to accept an offer or has almost but not quite decided.

When he or she is sitting on the fence, the fait accompli often provides the momentum for accepting the offer. Or it forces the customer to reject your offer. In either case, you've gotten valuable feedback on where you stand with the customer.

A Potpourri of Other Useful Tactics

Jujitsu tactic means you "step aside" and use the customer's strength to your advantage. Rather than defend your ideas, you invite criticism and advice, and you ask many questions. Questions are useful during a negotiation because they generate answers (including useful information about the customer's real interests), they don't offer a target for the customer to aim at, and they don't criticize (they educate—both you and the customer). Sincerely asked, such questions can diffuse a touchy situation and express a true desire on your part to negotiate in good faith. An example of a perfectly phrased jujitsu question is, "What concerns of yours am I neglecting to take into consideration?"

Shared interests tactic involves reminding the customer that you both have goals and interests in common. Expressing shared interests reinforces the win–win aspects of sales negotiating. Perhaps this tactic, more than any other, should be used generously throughout sales negotiations. It was stressed earlier that you should generally focus on interests, rather than positions, and you should articulate this frequently in your conversations. Sales negotiation is a delicate process and good salespeople constantly talk customer benefits, needs, common goals, and shared interests.

Reinforcement tactic means you bring in a third party (or parties), such as your manager, an operations specialist, a product manager, or corporate officer to (a) impress the customer that you're doing a lot to get his or her valuable business, (b) add strength (by numbers) to your cause, (c) be armed with backup help during negotiations, and (d) lend additional authority/"legitimacy" to your offers. While the importance of specific, high-level reinforcements is always helpful, just having numbers to support you provides a psychological advantage. This tactic is a must if the account is planning to bring a number of people to the negotiation; you need reinforcements to offset this advantage.

Forbearance tactic calls for holding off or stalling, rather than giving in immediately to the customer's request. The logic is that if you give in too quickly (even if you know you will ultimately have to), it will give the customer a psychological advantage and also establish a precedent as negotiations continue. Forbearance, on the other hand, will add to the value of your product/service in the customer's mind.

Deadlining tactic is a method in which you take the upper hand by getting the customer to agree to take action by a certain date in order to receive some special benefit. The deadline provides an incentive to act now and implies the offer will be withdrawn soon. In a sense, you are trading the special benefit or incentive for the customer's agreeing to the deadline.

KEY POINTS REVISITED

The sales negotiating strategy is both complex and free form so it's pertinent to review some key points:

1. Sales negotiating is a strategy, not a one-stop or piecemeal encounter with your customer. As a result, it requires planning, analysis, scheming, and careful implementation. There's nothing tricky about it, just lots of thinking, creativity, and good use of your sales skills.

2. You can and should initiate this strategy to accomplish your sales objectives and to overcome major blockades. If the customer suddenly asks to negotiate, postpone the negotiation until you can get a handle on all the issues, prepare adequately, and determine if it is in your best interest to negotiate at all.

3. The actual negotiation, like selling, should be challenging and fun. Arm yourself with appropriate negotiating tactics, use them well to position your trades, and remember that sales negotiating must be collaborative at all costs.

4. Finally, and most importantly, remember the basic premise behind professional sales negotiating: when you give something up, try to get something of equal value in return. That's the real definition of win–win.

6

CHAPTER

Access Strategy

ACCESS: THE STRATEGY THAT DEFINES ITSELF

If the access strategy didn't exist, it would have to be invented. The strategy is simply gaining access to key players to obtain their support in pursuit of your sales goals. Easier said than done! In sales jargon, *access* means getting the right message to the right people, with the right frequency, and with the right result! Is it an important strategy? You bet! To underline the importance of this critical strategy, think about some symptoms of "lost" sales or near misses:

- The "wrong" decision maker was the focus of your sales efforts.
- You could never figure out the account's decision process or the maze of people involved.
- It was impossible to get to the key players who ultimately made the decision.
- A "hidden" influencer suddenly "came out of the woodwork" to upset a decision that was in your favor.
- You were selling at one level when your competition was focused on a higher level.
- Your efforts were blocked by a low-level player who had more influence than you thought.

- Someone you "overlooked" in the decision maze shot down your proposal.
- Your proposal went all the way to the top of the organization before it was rejected.
- You simply never were able to pinpoint *why* you lost a piece of business.

If any of these symptoms sound familiar, chances are you were victimized because you couldn't effectively utilize an access strategy. Like any strategy, it takes time; however, an effective access strategy is a critical tool for selling to complicated organizations and their multiple decision makers. Without open access, the salesperson must rely on instinct and tactical selling, which often leads to lost opportunities. This strategy, unlike many others, should be utilized to various degrees with most major accounts, and it will certainly enhance and become a part of other strategies covered in this book.

THE ACCESS STRATEGY MODEL

In our experience, most sales managers and salespeople understand the reasons for gaining access, but few are able to reach sufficient depth—into the heart of the account organization. That's what access is all about. If you think of your own organization for a moment and include the politics, power, personalities, decision processes, and so on, you probably know it pretty well. You've analyzed it unconsciously by being part of the experience on an ongoing basis. To understand a major or complicated account, a similar process is needed to provide understanding, focus, and direction, so you can look in each nook and cranny and analyze how to best gain access. Once this picture is obtained, you then use a variety of selling tactics to penetrate the organization and gain access. Let's begin with the access strategy model in Exhibit 6.1.

The first tactic, *identify key players,* is a process of "scoping out" the account and may require research of different kinds. This first tactic or step may be relatively easy for an account that you've been selling for a number of years. However, it may cause you to revisit some key players to assess their changing roles and influence or even uncover others in the decision maze.

The second tactic, *analyze the decision maze,* requires in-depth study. In this step, you put together an organizational "snapshot" of the account to identify individual behavior and authority and to assess the linkages and relationships between different people. Here you begin to evolve your game plan for gaining access.

EXHIBIT 6–1

The third tactic, *gain access,* is where the action occurs, using selling skills and tactics to execute an access game plan. Depending on the organizational map, you employ a variety of tactics to establish links and gain visibility at different levels. We will refer to these different tactics, many of which you might be doing piecemeal, as subtactics. To optimize the impact, however, these subtactics need to be executed as part of a total access strategy. It's the only way true access can be obtained so that your regular sales skills can take over and drive the momentum to the ultimate sale. We'll cover the three tactics in depth.

☐ Tactic 1: Identify Key Players

While you may have a good fix on who's who in your major account(s), you may not have sorted them out by degree of influence relative to your goal achievement. To identify the people and fit them into the proper influence level, it's necessary to identify their roles. In brief, there are four traditional roles: ratifier, decision maker, influencer, and gatekeeper.

The ratifier (there can be more than one) is someone at a very high level in the organization who has low involvement in the decision process—by choice. However, this person can support or derail a decision. As a result, it is critical that the salesperson understand the ratifier's goals and the direction he or she wants to take the organization. Unfortunately, the presence of a salesperson is frequently perceived as adding little value to any decision-making interaction, however slight, with a ratifier. This is because the ratifier does not want to be involved in the decision-making process. Certainly not every decision requires a ratifier, but it's dangerous to overlook his or her presence and power. In terms of position, the ratifier is found at the vice presidential or presidential level.

The decision maker, while the easiest player to define, is perhaps the most illusive to pinpoint, unless you have had prior and consistent experience with him or her making defined types of decisions. This identification can be complicated because the decision process is often blurred. The decision makers often contribute to this confusion by letting their egos get in the way; they maintain self-esteem by claiming to be *the* decision maker. Compounding the situation is the fact that in today's marketplace environment, multiple decision makers for most major decisions are a fact of life, and committee decisions abound. Company politics play a role also; as people fight for turf, decision-making authority becomes more fuzzy. As a result, salespeople are constantly challenged to find other methods to determine who has the decision-making power and to cut through the misleading signals and frequent changes.

The influencers include anybody who can have a positive or negative impact on the decision. Because of their nebulous contribution, it's necessary to go one step further and categorize the degree of influence they exert. While this degree of influence can never be precisely measured, a broad ranking such as A (high), B (moderate), and C (low) will be very helpful when you launch your access plan. We'll come back to influence-ranking later in this chapter.

Finally, we come to gatekeepers, the people who don't have the authority to make strategic-type decisions but can block your access to those who can. The gatekeeper is often your initial contact on a specific inquiry, and his or her role is to screen out products and services that do not meet specifications. The gatekeeper rarely can say yes to anything but has the power to say no. The gatekeepers are people such as purchasing agents, legal counsel, lower-level users. While gatekeepers can also be influencers, their real power lies in deciding who to eliminate and who may gain further access. Don't confuse gatekeepers with secretaries, assistants, or receptionists, whose main goal is to screen you from reaching their bosses. Your approach in dealing with these "blockers" is quite different, and since this challenge is Selling 101, basic and nonstrategic, we won't deal with it here.

IDEA

PUT THE ORGANIZATION UNDER A MICROSCOPE

You may have a fix on many of your regular contacts (you'll get a reality check later in this chapter), but if you're thinking about broadening your sphere of access (and influence) you will need more in-depth information about decision makers, influencers, and ratifiers. You can accomplish this through intensive account research and study.

Tony Crimmins, an account rep for a high-tech manufacturer of networking systems, doubled his predecessor's business with a major account in one year. Tony accomplished many things, but he felt the most significant strategy he employed was identifying the real decision makers in this account.

When he first took over, he made a mission of analyzing the account's organization. By reading annual reports, company newsletters, and articles about the company and by constantly interviewing/probing each of his contacts (influencers and decision makers), he gradually built insight into who made the key decisions in his product area. Not surprisingly, he uncovered new buying sources (and decision makers) and found an ongoing budget that could be allocated to his product.

As a by-product of his intensive research, he also learned more about corporate goals and objectives and how his products could help satisfy the account's long-range business needs. His predecessor had apparently been content to grow the account at a good (but lower) rate, but Tony had higher ambitions and used the access strategy to open up new and bigger opportunities.

☐ Tactic 2: Analyze the Decision Maze

When relationships are referred to in this section, they do not mean your relationship with each individual. The assumption is that experienced, professional salespeople know how to build relationships with customers. But few salespeople know how to successfully navigate the corporate maze to access the key decision makers and hidden influencers. That's where the other type of relationship plays a role. The "relationship" we'll deal with here is how each account person relates to his peers and to the corporate decision process. These are critical relationships to analyze and understand, since they become the key to accessing the organization decision structure. Each of these factors needs to be mapped out so you can graphically comprehend decision power and its flow, then plan your strategic moves.

In Exhibit 6.2, you'll find a sample of a key player influencer chart that serves as a graphic for analyzing a hypothetical organization's decision interactions. While this organizational mapping can be done in different ways, it's important to recognize that some type of graphic is needed to pinpoint and focus the decision power; a picture is needed to make the connections between players. You'll see the importance of this later when we move into access sales tactics.

As indicated in the first tactic, identify key players, it's important to do some preliminary study to go beyond your normal span of contact and seek out the hidden players. This requires lots of objectivity, creativity, and old-fashioned digging (probing and study) to locate the "treasure." Once accomplished, the second step in this tactic, analyze the decision maze, is inserting the names (or initials) and titles in the appropriate boxes, as shown in Exhibit 6.2. In this worksheet, we show six levels of players: ratifiers, decision makers, influencers (A,B,C, indicating how much influence), and gatekeepers. This requires much more thought than simply filling in the boxes. It forces you to think and rethink who is involved in the decision process, and, equally important, how you can gain or increase (decrease) access to key people within an account. These are only preliminary placements, and, as you reveal additional information and relationships, various key players may move up and down the chart. Following are some critical assessments that need to be made before you can convert this chart into a dynamic and productive action plan. These factors follow as a series of questions that you should ask yourself.

How Frequently Am I Seeing Each Key Player?

According to most experts, the most realistic predictor of sales success is call frequency. While many sales executives feel that the quality of presentation is important, it's a fact of life that call frequency (constant access) provides exposure, builds relationships, offers many selling opportunities, and so on. The frequency is the key to access, but even where access is abundantly available, many salespeople rely on instinct for allocating their calls, possibly spending time with people they're comfortable with or by distributing calls equally (seeing everyone they can see on each visit). We'll deal with this allocation issue later, but the first step in making changes is to assess (1) who can be seen, (2) the frequency with

EXHIBIT 6.2

Sample Key Player Influencer Chart

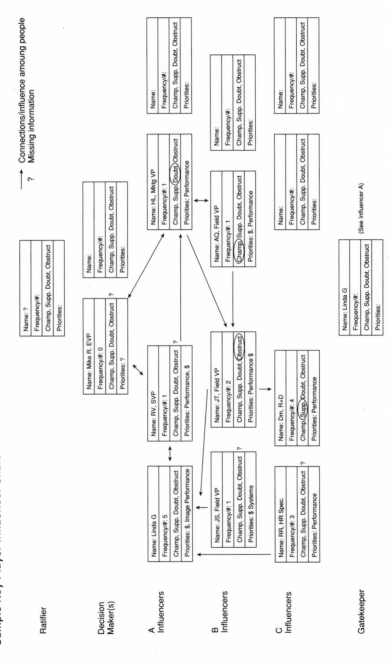

which they are currently visited, and (3) who you are unable to access. This can be measured on a weekly, monthly, or quarterly basis. In our sample chart in Exhibit 6.2, for example, the current frequency is based on monthly visits or appointments. Mike R., executive vice president, is not being seen at all, as indicated by the 0 on the frequency line in Mike's access box.

What Is Each Player's Degree of Commitment?

In analyzing the account players, it's important to assess each person's degree of commitment to your products, services, company, and to you personally. It's equally essential to determine how persuasive each player can be in influencing others. There are two dominant and interacting factors or behaviors that help accomplish this assessment. Similar to reading decision makers (READ profile) before a group presentation in implementing the team selling strategy, we utilize two of the behaviors, dynamics and receptivity, so that they interact with one another to identify four degrees of commitment. Please refer to the composite in Exhibit 6.3.

For example, someone who is low in receptivity and high in dynamics is labeled an obstructionist; he or she has the persuasiveness and negative receptivity to cause problems. At the opposite corner, the decision maker or influencer with high dynamics and high receptivity has the potential to become a champion for your products and for you. More about how to access and capitalize on these degrees of commitment will come later. For now, let's merely describe how these four quadrants work together.

On the vertical axis is dynamics. By dynamics, we mean how able the person is to influence others to his or her point of view. A person's dynamics can be anywhere from low to high.

On the horizontal axis is receptivity, which defines how supportive the person is of you, your company, and your goals—anywhere from low to high. Definitions of the four degrees of commitment are as follows:

- *Champion*—A person who is high in receptivity and dynamics; someone who'll go to bat for you, who will actively support you by influencing other people in the account.
- *Supporter*—Someone high in receptivity but lower in dynamics. This person is receptive, but, because his or her dynamics in the organization are lower, this person is less likely to influence others on your behalf.

E X H I B I T   6 . 3

Four Degrees of Commitment

- *Doubter*—Someone low in receptivity and dynamics. This person is not particularly supportive of you (or may be supportive of a competitor or the status quo), but won't do too much damage. Since his or her dynamics in the organization are low, the likelihood of highly influencing others is slim.
- *Obstructionist*—This person is nonreceptive and is high in dynamics. Likely to be vociferous, he or she may opt to either support a competitor or the status quo, block you, or both.

When we get to the access tactics, you'll see the importance of assessing the players' degree of commitment. For now, the objective is to identify the possible behavior. If you were using a worksheet or document like Exhibit 6.2, you would insert the appropriate behavior in each player's box as we did. You should recognize that we are building a profile of each person so we can eventually use this map as a springboard for connecting them. This will enable you to access key people more frequently, get to see those players that have been inaccessible in the past, visit those you have overlooked, or focus more calls where you can get a better return on investment for your effort.

What Are the Key Players' Priorities?
One important linkage we'll try to use in connecting decision makers is each individual's priorities. Priority, as it is used here, refers to a business concern (not personal interest). As you learned in basic selling, if you can identify a need and satisfy it, you're on the way to a sale. This is a simplification of what's needed here, and we have to go beyond product/service needs and focus on identifying business priorities. Fortunately, the job is made easier because there are a limited number of

business concerns (priorities). The small number of priorities makes your job easier when you start to analyze the maze and seek common denominators that you can use to establish connections.

While you might not use our labels or be concerned with all of these, here are seven major business priorities that are generic to most organizations and the decision makers in each:

- *Image:* how well the service/product enhances the image/reputation of the decision maker's organization.
- *Financial:* the economic aspects of the purchase: cost, price, profitability, leasing, terms.
- *Performance:* how well the service/product performs, what results can be expected for the decision maker and end users (output, maintenance, ease of use).
- *Pull-through:* a concern with what you can offer to help the customer resell your products (merchandising, advertising, distributor sales rep training, etc.). This priority is appropriate for companies that sell their products to resellers (channels) like retailers or distributors.
- *Relationship:* how well the sales professional and his or her "team" work with the decision maker and his or her "team"; this may be of a professional or personal nature.
- *Service:* any services, regular or special, you offer—delivery, sources of market or industry information, providing free labor for resets or inventory, consulting services.
- *Systems:* how well the service/product fits in with current systems, procedures, policies (compatibility, installation, training).

How do you identify which priority is most important to each decision maker or influencer? Ask. While questioning is considered a core selling skill, I'd be remiss if I didn't remind the reader that you need to ask open-ended questions subtly and frequently on many sales calls. (That's why access is considered a strategy, not a piecemeal tactic!) You may be wondering about the people to whom you have no access. How do you identify their needs? One approach is to ask peers and subordinates (as well as superiors) what other decision makers' concerns or priorities are. For example, you might say: "Mary, how does Charley feel about the installation? Is it meeting *his* performance objectives?"

RED FLAG

BEWARE OF DISINGENUOUS RESPONSES

If the word *disingenuous* caught your attention, that's good. It's a term used by attorneys and indicates a lack of candor or a false appearance of simple frankness; *calculating* might be a synonym. Many salespeople are too trusting of their customers and contacts in accounts, and this is particularly true when asking penetrating questions about sensitive issues such as decision-making authority, priorities, and influence, among others. As indicated, many players don't want to admit they don't have power; others prefer to cover the facts with a smoke screen.

Some salespeople accept as accurate and true the disingenuous responses of customers and contacts, and often such information can be misleading. No matter how good your questioning skills are, or even if you trust your customers 100 percent, beware. They are going to mislead you or try to cover up when they don't have an answer (or don't want to share the *right* answer). Remember, these are fuzzy, intangible concepts that overlap, and you will get subjective opinions or disingenuous answers.

The only solution is to not accept any single response about authority, company politics or culture, influence, power, or decision making. Instead, after tactfully probing for pertinent information from one person, check out the information you garnered with at least two or three other players. By validating those initial responses with players at different levels, you will come a lot closer to pinpointing individual influence and decision-making power.

Collecting information at every level is a critical selling skill, but organizing it into a chart or format is the bottom line. The information doesn't have to be perfect, but it should be reasonably accurate so you can analyze it with confidence. Naturally, this takes time, effort, and planning, but these are characteristics of the sales strategist!

How to Analyze the Relationships between Players

Up to this point, you've been able to map out the profile of the organization decision process and the individual players. Regardless of whether you have used the mapping procedure in Exhibit 6.2 or some other suitable method for charting, it's time to start targeting people and tactics for access. In brief, you seek a variety of clues for gaining access to:

1. *Individuals who are at the ratifier, decision maker, influencer levels (particularly influencer A) to whom you have no access.* Anyone at a high level to whom you do not have access must become an access target. These high-placed players can sink or support a proposal quickly. Not knowing whose side they are on is extremely dangerous. If nothing else surfaces from this second tactic, analyze the decision maze, this step is still worth the time and effort. This is the critical output from mapping the account's decision tree and levels of influence, and it will certainly reinforce (or identify) people you need to access. Accessing them is another challenge, but we'll deal with the sales tactics that can make that happen later.

2. *Individuals at the same high levels to whom you already have access but whom you need to see more frequently.* This gap may not be as obvious to you as someone to whom you have been denied access. However, if you look over the chart, in general, and particularly at the decision maker and influencer levels, the higher levels should be seen more frequently than the lower levels. In reality, the opposite is true in most accounts. In other words, salespeople have a tendency to visit with people who are more accessible, those with whom they have relationships, and the ones with whom they transact business (orders, service, user support). While you can't ignore these C influencers and gatekeepers, you should recognize that you have a limited number of sales calls to invest in an account. In other words, you should get the best ROI (return on investment) from each call by "spending" the calls where you will optimize the return.

No one can give you a perfect or permanent guideline for allocating your calls among the various players in an account, but the Pareto law supplies a good benchmark. Pareto, a management engineer, discovered a concept that has been applied (and validated) to many activities. When applied to sales effort, it indicates you should be spending about 65 percent of your sales calls with decision makers and A influencers, about 20 percent of your calls with B influencers, and 15 percent of your calls invested in C influencers (including gatekeepers). To reinforce the point, take heed of what Willie Sutton, the infamous bank robber, said when asked why he robbed banks. He quickly replied: "Because that's where the money is!" This serves as a metaphor for calling at high levels: That's where the decisions are made.

Using Pareto's law as a guideline or benchmark may suggest that sometimes the frequency of sales calls needs to be changed—increased in some instances, decreased in others.

3. *Players who need to be influenced in a positive manner, through your selling or through people inside the organization.* If you've done your homework on the four levels of influence for each of the players, you'll have a good idea who the champions, supporters, doubters, and obstructionists are. This will help you in a number of ways.

First, it will underline how immediately (and frequently) you need to reach decision makers who are not at the champion or supporter level, or those whose relative decision-making power is in question. In your assessment of relationships and influence, you should look for connections between players that can be capitalized on to influence decisions (similar priorities, reporting relationships, personal relationships, if known). In Exhibit 6.2, for example, you'll see arrows connecting people who can affect each other's thought processes (and decision input). Some of the arrows indicate reporting relationships, some show peer relationships (i.e., the possibility of a champion influencing an obstructionist), others indicate situations where a few people can impact on another. Other relationships might suggest common priorities or business concerns. Finally, and most importantly, arrows can help you network your way to the top—by indicating people to help you over the human hurdles and obstacles on your way up the ladder.

🚩 **RED FLAG**

DON'T TRY TO DO THIS MENTALLY!

What's the point of this mapping or organization charting? First, you can't do this mentally because in the typical business sales situation today, you have 5 to 10 (or more) persons who influence every major transaction or commitment. When you add in all the elements you need to analyze (four to five pieces of information that are critical to each individual), you will need to visualize perhaps 50 pieces of information and then draw connections between people. Obviously, this amounts to an impossible job to do casually or in your head. You need a map or worksheet to graphically portray the organizational influence as it relates to your products/services. You also need a worksheet to plot your moves or tactics. Having said that, let's move on to the sales tactics that you can employ to overcome obstacles and capitalize on opportunities.

◇ Tactic 3: Gain Access

Gaining access, as a tactic, is really a potpourri of selling tactics. Like negotiating tactics, you're dealing with moving targets, a variety of people and situations, which defy a smooth formula or pat solution. As in other strategies, this is the point at which tactical sales skills take over. You can arm yourself with a variety of approaches, but each decision is dictated by your assessment of the individual based on your past experiences and current feedback (observations or perceptions provided by others). However, the tactics you utilize should include gaining access (and, if the information is available, prior call frequency, level of influence, degree of commitment, priorities, and connections you or others can make). This requires matching and scheming, putting a plan into play, and, most importantly, gaining access strategically (as opposed to piecemeal sales calls and attempts). Recognize that the tactics described below work best when they are part of a total plan. Like a game, moves, adjustments, advances, retreats, and countermoves need to be made to achieve access objectives. A strategy creates synergism; the end result (sum) will be much greater than the individual moves (if done piecemeal). The bottom line is that if one tactic doesn't work, another will. When enough tactics have worked, you will have gained access to the right people. Some of the tactics that follow are situational, while others are designed to deal with decision makers with varying degrees of commitment.

Coach tactic involves finding a "friend in court" who can help you gain access and do related internal intelligence work for you. The best candidate for a coach is a champion or a supporter who has a stake in the final outcome for which you're striving.

The coach gives you feedback on progress, competition, and, as it relates to access, "where the bodies are buried." He or she can provide endless information on how decisions are made, who influences whom, and in some instances can even arrange entrée to hard-to-access players. How do you identify and develop a coach? In most sales situations, you'll generally find people (at the influencer level) who want your product/service or who like you and your organization. As you proceed through your sales cycle, you recognize these individuals' needs or desires to be involved in a positive way. You don't have to be a psychologist to realize that coaches have varying motives for involvement; they either want to look good themselves, feel that you are the right fit for their organization, or personally like you. In every case, they are more responsive to your questions and offer lots of positive comments. You need to initiate this interplay subtly, of course, and build a supportive and ongoing relationship. You maintain this relationship by more frequent contact and by providing the coach with information on your progress and asking for help on potential problems.

A few years ago, one of Porter Henry & Company's sales reps had been working for almost a year with an account that had major potential for us. Our sales rep, having established a relationship with a coach who felt the strong need for sales training for the account's sales force, nurtured this relationship for six months and was able to access and influence a number of key people. Although suddenly transferred to a new job 250 miles away, the coach was still helpful, continuing to provide guidance and influence people. Without such help, we probably would not have been able to access the right people and sell the account.

A final word on the coach tactic: Make the coach look good at every turn of the sales cycle. Give the coach credit for ideas, suggestions, and for identifying needs and problems.

Network tactic requires you to use every connection and method for making strategic contacts. Effective networkers use every method they can think of to reach the right people. For example, they get other players to introduce them to those they need to access; they arrange to meet key players at public functions (conferences, social events, professional organizations, charity events); or they get a friend or contact to set up a social lunch. There is no limit to the number of techniques that can be used to network around an organization and meet key people. These ploys or subtactics include:

- Have a higher-level person from your company call him or her to set the stage for a visit from you.
- Invite the "hidden" player to be a guest (or even a guest speaker) at a function.
- Set up a meeting as a short, fact-finding mission, rather than a sales call.
- Invite him or her to attend a business meeting, such as a business review or other type of formal presentation.
- Use your coach to get you an appointment.

Network tactic is a free form process for gaining access and is limited only by your creativity in linking people together. The key, however, is not merely meeting people, but on staying focused—to *whom* must you gain access? This focus can emanate only from a strategic plan.

Top-gun selling tactic is reserved for the ratifier or decision maker. The biggest challenge in multilevel selling is gaining access to high-level people, the "top guns." While the experts will tell you that the ideal selling scenario is to enter the organization at the top level, in practice this is not always possible (or desired). However, influencing the top guns is critical to your success, and you can't leave it to chance or rely on subordinates to carry the message (and/or be persuasive in doing it). Assuming you can set an appointment (without stepping on a subordinate's toes), you have two options: (1) Handle the call (or calls) yourself or (2) bring along someone from your organization at a similar level to the account decision maker. The latter may be a good way to get a hard-to-come-by appointment, but in either case you face the same issues. In brief, you need to accomplish a number of call objectives dictated by the top gun's preferences. Top guns tend to be:

- Big-picture oriented.
- Not interested in product.
- Future focused.
- Interested in trends.
- Concerned about growth and profit issues.

It's critical to hit some or all of these hot buttons while building relationships, increasing support, demonstrating your knowledge of his or her organization and needs. The top-gun call requires heavy planning. Above all, it requires two simple elements that are best described by the phrase "Give and get." In other words, you need to provide some information of value and receive some in return. It's a certainty there will be no product selling with the top gun.

What can you *give?* You need to provide some value related to the top gun's needs and interests. For example, you can supply information on industry trends, plans that your company is making that will affect the top gun's long-range goals, a specific issue that may be affecting the account's profits, a potential problem about which the top gun may not be aware, research from your company or the industry. You generally do not discuss specific products or a major commitment that you are seeking at lower levels. However, there are two exceptions. One is when you know the top gun is a hands-on executive and this decision is important to his or her goals and objectives. The other is related to selling major concepts, such as an alignment or partnership arrangement, which will be covered in the next chapter. If you have validated that the top gun is involved, then it makes sense to subtly lead into the product purchase if the discussion moves in that direction. If this happens, stick with the big-picture and stay away from mundane features and benefits. Generally, the top gun will not want to talk about the specific details of a proposal, although he or she may want some feedback on how a project is moving along.

What can you *get?* You'll want to get something tangible from the top gun during your presentation. You should plan your questions carefully. You need to know what his or her priorities are, where the organization is headed, what his or her perspective is, opinions on past initiatives, and, if your organizations have had an ongoing relationship, how he or she perceives the situation.

Not every decision involves a ratifier or decision maker, but the best salespeople recognize that they need to have access to all the top guns. Even if you only see these people infrequently you will gain visibility and reinforce your presence when they supply input for major decisions.

ACCESS TACTICS FOR DEALING WITH FOUR LEVELS OF COMMITMENT

Players at different levels such as champion, supporters, doubters, and the obstructionist may be easy or difficult to access. If they are available, they can also be used to access other key people. The tactics on the next pages focus on these interacting challenges.

The champion is already in your corner, and the assumption is that you have access as needed. Therefore, the champion should be your key to gaining access at other levels. As indicated earlier, the champion may be an ideal coach for you, and you will probably accomplish everything you need if you can make this transition. If not, the champion can still be of great help. To keep your champion motivated, make certain that you reinforce how he or she will benefit. In addition, encourage the champion to open doors for you and to sell internally. However, don't take him or her for granted; provide both rewards and information to keep your strongest ally in your corner.

The supporter doesn't need a lot of attention, unless you are trying to move him or her to a greater commitment as with the champion. The supporter can be extremely helpful in convincing doubters to change their position and will be less overwhelming than a champion in accomplishing this end. As with the champion, the supporter's efforts need to be constantly reinforced.

Doubters are always a potential problem, and you need to focus a degree of your call allocation on selling them. Ask questions to determine the source of the doubt, and zero in on business and personal priorities. One of your objectives is to move them to the supporter level. If possible, modify your approach or proposal to give them some "ownership."

Obstructionists, as you can imagine, are a real problem; you must keep an eye out for damage they can create. Beyond that, you need to take a more proactive role in converting the obstructionists to your side or minimizing the destruction they can effect. If the obstructionists are on a low influence level, you probably can contain the problem; however, don't ignore them, since this may create more animosity or encourage the obstructionists to influence others more aggressively. If you know the obstructionist's priority (for example, financial) and have a supporter with the same priority, this may lend itself to some "influence selling." If the supporter is willing to go to bat for you, first review the financial benefits so he or she is armed for the meeting with the obstructionists.

⚑ RED FLAG

DEVELOP A TACTICAL ACCOUNT PLAN

With all the players involved, the mix of levels and priorities, shifting call frequencies, various selling tactics, and a host of objectives, you have a lot to manage in penetrating an important account. To compound the dilemma, you have to manage the changes that you create (selling, making progress, building relationships, etc.). You also have to recognize and deal with the change within the account organization: people moving into new jobs and leaving the organization, the dynamics of personalities, corporate culture and politics, and so on. In addition to the myriad of potential changes mentioned above, you also need to allocate and execute individual sales calls and other contacts (telephone, correspondence). Without a plan (which must also change frequently), you'll be relying on instinct to make all this work for you. This could prove very risky, given all the events, people, activities, and forces that need to be coordinated and organized into a cohesive access plan. What's needed is a simple and flexible weekly or monthly plan that reflects your changing call allocation and tactical needs. If you try to manage this complex process in your head, you're doomed to miss key opportunities and connections, and you're bound to have some of the tactics fall between the cracks. You don't need a short-term action for every account, but for key accounts that you have targeted for further penetration, it's a must. A sample of this type of tactical action plan can be found in Exhibit 6.4.

EXHIBIT 6.4

Sample Access Strategy Tactical Plan

Key Player	Objectives	Tactics
RV	■ Ask Linda to talk with RV ■ Get appointment	■ List of benefits to RV
HL	■ Have AQ influence HL	■ Stress performance benefits ■ Send related article (Times, 8/24)
AQ	■ Provide feedback on progress	■ Buy lunch and thank for help

As you must realize by now, gaining access is a thinking person's strategy. It requires selling tactics or skills, most of which good salespeople do instinctively. The real challenge of the access strategy is cognitive: Your thinking capacity enables you to analyze the account organization in terms of individual players and relationships, to identify possible linkages, and then to design an organized strategic plan of attack. The tactical implementation is done with the same amount of work you normally do for the targeted account. The difference is that you use more tactics, focusing your efforts on calls and meetings in which you can generate a better return on investment (and time) for each call.

7

The Alignment Strategy

ALIGNMENT: A DYNAMIC AND CHALLENGING FORCE

If climbing a mountain were a metaphor for implementing strategies, the alignment strategy would surely be near the peak. It's the most challenging to use and achieve, although it's not a strategy for everyone or every account! Alignment is a function of matching organization needs and capabilities (your company's and the customer's). Like a good partnership, it requires intimate knowledge sharing, solid relationships, and a powerful commitment from both parties. While you may use the strategy only on rare occasions or not at all, your knowledge and execution of it, in part, will provide you with significant payback, regardless. As in our metaphor for climbing a mountain, you may start out climbing Mt. Everest, for example, and never reach the top. Even though you reach only the 10,000-foot level, you still receive significant benefits—a sense of accomplishment, exercise, conditioning, adventure, and so on. The alignment strategy is like climbing a mountain, not only because it can provide huge rewards, but also because of the challenges along the way. And even if you don't get to the partner level (the peak), you will gain many benefits in the process, including growing your business.

ALIGNMENT STRATEGY DEFINED

Webster defines *alignment* as: "Being or coming into precise adjustment or correct relative position; an arrangement of groups or forces in relation to one another." The alignment strategy feeds off this definition: A long-term plan or approach to select and build an appropriate relationship between the sales organization and the account organization that will achieve both organizations' goals.

If this isn't the top of the mountain, then what is? If this sounds vague, general, or confusing, bear with me since this chapter will put "flesh on the bones." This is a very conceptual, creative, and challenging strategy that can provide rewards at every level. The definition will become more clear as we examine specific levels in the next section. However, keep in mind that there are a number of criteria for using this strategy. They are:

- A good working knowledge of other strategies (discussed in Chapters 2 to 5), since they become important substrategies in gaining an alignment.
- An alignment "offering," a concept defined by your company, or one you can shape to capitalize on the strengths of both organizations.
- The right type of customer or account, who will be receptive to alignment to gain mutual benefits.
- The patience and vision to see the alignment opportunity emerging over time.

Having said that, let's move on to the various levels of alignment.

FIVE LEVELS OF ALIGNMENT

If you assess your current position or level of penetration with a variety of accounts, you should recognize a hierarchy of steps. Your perceptions may not agree exactly with these five steps or levels, but I trust you'll agree that there is a series of levels indicating various types of account relationships.

The shaded sphere represents you and your organization. The large A sphere is the account organization, and the lines represent a sales relationship.

Spectator

You and your organization have no sales relationship with the account. The account deals with your competitors, does not see a need for your products and services, or you choose not to work with the account.

Vendor

You and your competitors are on a relatively equal playing field, supplying products and services to the account.

Preferred Provider

You are the supplier of choice and own the largest share (or total share) of the account's business. You advise the account on your products and services.

Business Consultant

You help the customer manage a portion of its business. You consult with the customer to help meet its long-term business goals.

Partner (Ally)

You and your organization *manage* the account's business in your area of expertise, providing bottom line value that it cannot achieve without you. You are considered to be an integral part of the account's organization. You provide completely integrated systems to run the operation, and the product mix is often composed of your products and services, and your competitors'.

Another way of delineating these five levels is to break them out on a spreadsheet as in Exhibit 7.1.

As you review Exhibit 7.1, you should draw a few other conclusions. As you climb closer to becoming an ally or partner, the three indicators of progress—relationship, access, and resources—grow in linear fashion. In other words, to reach the partner/ally level (full alignment), you need to have a strong organization-to-organization relationship, close

E X H I B I T   7 . 1

Common Characteristics of Five Levels of Alignment

	Organization to Organization Relationship	Access	Resources Provided
Spectator	Sales organization provides no products or services	Limited, usually to gatekeepers	Few or none
Vendor	Sales organization provides products and/or services	Limited; usually lower levels, including gatekeepers	Product is most important resource; value-added services often provided
Preferred Provider	Sales organization provides products and/or services	Access to low and middle levels	Products and value-added services
Business Consultant	Sales organization provides consulting to help account meet business goals	Access to all or most levels	Products, value-added services, consulting beyond products
Partner/Ally	Sales organization manages a function of account's business; often contractual, though may be nonbinding	Access to all or most levels	Two organizations share and manage resources, including those of the account and the sales organization's

to 100 percent access at most levels, and a sharing of resources. This chart also reinforces the fact that you normally start at the spectator level with most accounts and gradually improve your position within the account, moving from level to level—if the conditions are right and there is a good match. Similar to mountain climbing, you start at the bottom and, while you may set a goal to reach a reasonable level, you probably don't set your sights for the top until you have ascended to a major height. At this point, you can catch your breath, sense the full possibilities, and then go for it! Later, we'll provide some examples that will help clarify the alignment strategy further. Except for the spectator level, any of the other positions or levels may work for you and meet your account goals. How you position yourself depends on your goals and your company focus. In other words, if your objective is to be a strong vendor in all of your accounts (or even a preferred provider), that's OK. You don't have to "go for it" (the peak) to use this strategy.

WHAT'S YOUR AQ?

Would you like to gauge your alignment quotient (AQ), or alignment level, for one of your accounts? If so, focus on one of your good, high-potential accounts and use it as a profile for responding to the eight categories that follow.

What's Your AQ?
An Alignment Quotient Indicator
For each of the eight categories below (A through H), circle the number of the statement that best describes the situation with your profiled account.

A. *1.* This account has relationships with very few people from my organization.

2. I and/or others in my organization can get access to key players in the account on an as-needed basis a good deal of the time.

3. I and/or others in my organization have open access to most of the key players in the account.

4. I and/or others in my organization have open access to all the key players, including higher-level executives, in the account.

B. *1.* This account tends to bring me into the decision process at the later stages, often after many of the larger business decisions have already been made.

2. This account brings me in during the fairly early stages of the decision process.

3. This account often seeks advice and input from me and/or others in my organization as it develops plans and strategies.

4. This account relies on me/my organization to develop plans and strategies for it for the area of its business in which we have expertise.

C. *1.* This account tends to be rather closemouthed about its "internal" information and plans; account decision makers tend to treat purchases as onetime events.

2. This account tends to put its buying objectives on any given sale into the context of its larger business goals.

Alignment Quotient Indicator (continued)

   3. I have specific knowledge of this account's long- and short-term business goals and usually sell based on them (rather than purely on product or service benefits).

   4. I help the account set its business goals in my area of expertise—not just for my products and services, but for the entire business function/category.

D. 1. This account often plays one vendor against another and tends to use negotiating techniques such as "nibbling" or "good guy/bad guy."

   2. This account tends to treat all its vendors/suppliers equally.

   3. This account rarely, or never, makes unreasonable demands of me. It also looks out for my interests as well as its own.

   4. This account and my organization work together as business partners, almost always arriving at win–win outcomes.

E. 1. This account's buying decisions are highly price sensitive.

   2. This account emphasizes other features as well as cost in making purchase decisions.

   3. This account takes a "big-picture" view of working with me and/or other sales organizations, price (or other financial considerations) being but one of many decision-making factors.

   4. This account is rarely focused on the cost of products and services. Our success is measured by our ability to run a function of its business and to meet larger, long-term business goals related to cost reductions, profitability, etc.

F. 1. This account treats each sale as something I must earn anew.

   2. This account provides a fairly steady stream of business for me.

   3. This account provides a steady and growing stream of business for me.

   4. I ensure my own continued stream of business in the account by managing the account's business function/category judiciously and fairly, with the aim of meeting its long-term business goals.

G. 1. This account tends to view us as a vendor of goods or services.

   2. This account tends to view us as an organization that can fulfill its short-term product, service, or business needs.

   3. This account tends to view us as a consultant or a partner that helps it make business decisions in its best interests, especially regarding our products and services.

   4. This account gives us the responsibility of running a business function/ category from start to finish and managing our competitors' business within the account, as needed.

Alignment Quotient Indicator (concluded)

H. *1.* My organization tends to have a "one-size-fits-all" marketing or sales mentality, with the focus being on short-term, bottom-line dollars as the measure of success.

   2. Increasing our share of business within an account is a top priority for my organization.

   3. My organization allows some flexibility in providing our accounts with options and customized solutions, and focusing on mid- as well as short-term sales results.

   4. I consider my organization to be flexible and visionary. It encourages us to take creative approaches in offering customized solutions to achieve long-term business results for our accounts.

Now add up the totals for the numbers you've selected. Then score yourself as follows:

AQ Scoring:

8–12	Vendor
13–20	Preferred provider
21–29	Business consultant
30–32	Partner/ally

We hope this exercise helped you identify your level with a specific account. It should also enhance and clarify the definition of each level. While this chapter will focus primarily on the business consultant and partner/ally levels, it's important to recognize that (1) to reach any of the top three levels is an accomplishment in itself; (2) you may remain at any level due to your own goals or those of your company; and (3) to reach any level, you normally have to pass through the previous level. Most importantly, strategies are required to reach the top three levels, and your strategic action plans will include those strategies discussed previously. From now on, when we discuss the alignment strategy, it will focus primarily on reaching the two highest levels, business consultant or partner/ally.

EXAMPLES OF THE ALIGNMENT STRATEGY

The following are examples that will help you crystallize the concept further and enable you to determine how this strategy can be initiated with selected major customers or target accounts. Some of these real-life examples are mandated by a corporate strategy, while others are driven by individual salespeople who recognize opportunities and then shape their offering to capitalize on them.

- *Consumer packaged goods:* A grocery products company sells its accounts on a "category-management" concept whereby it assists in managing an entire category for a retail chain. For example, a toothpaste manufacturer manages the entire category of health and beauty aids, making decisions and recommendations regarding space allocations, inventory, product distribution—all indicators of profit.

- *Temporary personnel services:* A temporary personnel organization has carved out alignments with major accounts to set up shop inside the account. With a full-time manager operating from within the company, it manages the entire temp function. The manager provides all services for the acquisition and ongoing use of temporary employees in accordance with the company's needs, including selection, training, supervision, and testing. In addition, the in-house temp manager fills orders from competitors' temp inventory.

- *Computer data systems:* One company specifically builds and operates its clients' corporate data management centers. This requires equipment and personnel.

- *Training services:* One training company has empowered its salespeople to form alliances, wherever possible, with major accounts. In conducive situations, the salesperson will take the initiative to propose that the client outsource its total training facility or a segment of it. Once the partnership is established, the vendor manages the training, using its own products and selecting competitive products to shape its total curriculum.

- *Printing:* A printing vendor puts together a proposal to handle all of an account's printing needs. It has expanded its alignment to include supplying binders (which it purchases from a binder manufacturer) as well as collating, warehousing, and fulfillment of orders.

As you can see from these examples, alignments come in different shapes and sizes and potentially can, under the right conditions, be employed in most industries. However, there are certain common denominators for most of these alignment situations.

Business consultant and partner/ally are considered the highest levels of alignment because your organization and the account organization align and operate closely in a particular function or category of its business. You and your organization *help* or actually *manage* a piece of the account's business, a portion of its business where your organization has a particular expertise. In doing so, you provide bottom line value that it cannot achieve without you.

In both levels, you are considered to be an integral part of the account's operation, just as its own marketing, finance, or sales divisions are. In many cases, you not only both align with the account and manage a portion of its business, but you also manage your competitors' business in the account, as well. So your mix of products and services may be composed of your own as well as your competitors'.

This calls for great expertise on your part, a high level of commitment from the sales organization's management, a strategic corporate decision to move in this direction, and a significant investment in resources that you provide to the account. Often, the partner/ally relationship involves the account's outsourcing entire functions or departments.

This case study gives you a simplified snapshot of the complex inner workings of an alignment of this scope. Such a transaction takes significant time, many sales calls, in-depth planning, and much creativity.

If you assess the critical events that make this scenario possible, these are the important ones that should jump out at you:

- Working together, you and the customer as a team know more about a particular function of the customer's business than either of you would independently. This means your expertise and the customer's complement each other.

 C A S E   S T U D Y

CLIMBING THE ALIGNMENT MOUNTAIN

Jane Paterno is a key account manager for a major manufacturer of reproduction and facsimile equipment. In 10 years, she has moved from sales trainee to territory representative, and she has been in her current position for the past 5 years. One of her major accounts is Global Airlines, with most of its executive and administrative employees and key departments headquartered in one huge complex.

When Jane inherited the account, her company had about 20 percent of the installed equipment at Global. Five years later, she was the preferred provider and had a 42 percent share of this customer's business. The balance of the business was shared by one major competitor (about 20 percent) and a variety of smaller suppliers. She had worked hard on building relationships and selling at various levels to move from vendor to preferred provider. However, she wanted more business and determined that she might be able to double her share of Global's business if she could get it to standardize with her company's equipment. At present, each department was encouraged to purchase from her company when ordering new equipment or trading in older units, but this was difficult to track. There were 50 to 60 departments at headquarters, and most had multiple equipment installations. Jane had over 100 decision makers and influencers on her Global contact list, so it was obvious she couldn't cover all these people effectively enough to keep the competition out. She had built the account through hard work, but she felt she would plateau unless she could come up with another scheme.

In discussions with her boss, it became apparent they had to create a proposal that Global couldn't refuse and then sell it at higher levels. Jane recognized that profits and cash flow were major concerns for any airline, especially Global, which was expanding its grip on international routes. She was also aware that Global was driving for more internal efficiency and cost savings. Global was purchasing about $3 million worth of copying and fax equipment a year (including service contracts), and Jane decided to focus initially on cash flow. With expanded purchases, she knew she could provide additional discounts of about 10 percent, a $300,000 annual savings. She also thought her company would be able to service competitive equipment without compromising quality or service.

In discussing her concept with Jerome Brown, Global's assistant controller, she was advised that a potential savings of $300,000 was intriguing, but he believed that unless she could show a more substantial savings she'd have difficulty getting anyone's attention. Certainly, she would not be able to sell the concept to upper management. Back to the drawing board, Jane did some further research. Another possibility surfaced while she was visiting a busy department and noticed two or three people waiting to send faxes. During her calls at Global in the next few weeks, she noticed a similar problem at some (but not all) copier and fax stations. Sensing a potential savings for Global, she went back to her boss and sold him on getting their system analysts to do an equipment-usage study. The system analyst team picked 20 sites to study, noting personnel waiting-and-walking times (based on distance from equipment), and overall usage. Finally, they produced a brief report detailing recommendations for the sites studied, moving some

CASE STUDY concluded

machines (closer to heavy users), replacing some with faster models, noting excessive downtime while waiting for service. Based on average wages for administrative personnel and executives, Global's savings for the entire system (including competitive sites) were estimated at $125,000 annually.

Now feeling more confident about savings, Jane met again with Jerome Brown. Impressed with the potential for savings, Jerome once again made a suggestion. "You may not be aware of it, but we're also going through some reengineering here so we can be more competitive. I wonder how this change will impact our other departments—those that purchase equipment, or requisition service, even our internal systems." Jerome made a few internal calls and came up with an additional savings estimate of $100,000 *if* Jane's company would provide a full-time, in-house serviceperson to manage the equipment operation, service, and installation and to consult on new installations. Jane agreed to meet with each of the three department heads that Jerome had called to validate the savings and to ease any concerns they might have. Before she left that meeting, she indicated she would try to set this up as a plan for on-site service management, but she also asked if Jerome would be the champion for this project, if she were successful getting a go-ahead from her company. He agreed.

With her boss's tentative approval, Jane drafted a proposal of the entire plan, enabling both companies to align on this opportunity. Once it was approved by her boss, she got Jerome's buy-in, which resulted in his arranging individual appointments for Jane with two critical decision makers—Jerome's boss, the comptroller, and the vice president of finance. The vice president of finance, while basically satisfied with the proposal, objected to her company taking over the entire copying/fax servicing operations and making recommendations on new purchases. He believed the presence of a competitor would make Jane's company work harder, would keep pricing in line automatically, and could provide parts for competitive machines that weren't readily available. After negotiating the issue, Jane agreed to a reshaping of the proposal to include a 75–25 percent split in purchases and servicing between her company and the major competitor. In return, she asked for support from the vice president of finance in acquiring a two-year initial contract (rather than one, as proposed).

The final approval for the proposal was obtained as Jane, her boss, and the proposed in-house manager met with Global's executive committee to work through details and obtain final approval. As a result of her one-year campaign, Jane's company achieved a higher alignment with Global, taking over partial management of an operation, with $500,000-plus savings for Global, and a dramatic increase in business (almost double!).

- You can make more of a profit contribution to the customer's operation than if the customer or one of your competitors ran it alone. This means you make a unique contribution the customer can't get elsewhere.

- You can integrate the component parts, operations, and systems of the customer's business so they run seamlessly. This means you are a fully integrated element of the business operation.

- You can show bottom line value in enhancing the account's revenues and/or reducing costs. If you cannot, you will not be a partner because there will be no reason for you to have to manage, or help manage, the operation.

- The customer's culture and goals must be conducive to these kinds of business arrangements. It takes a great deal of trust and faith to allow someone else to run part of your business. It also requires a willingness to share costs, risks, and resources.

- There must be a compelling reason for the account to partner with you. Ordinarily, the compelling reason is a combination of many of the requirements we just covered.

RED   FLAG

WATCH OUT FOR THE BENDS IN THE ROAD

Unlike other strategies covered here, alignment strategy is eclectic. While it is quite different from other strategies, it also draws from the best of them. It would be hard to imagine any salesperson or sales manager successfully implementing the alignment strategy without employing some elements of consultative selling, team selling, access strategy, or negotiating strategy, or without selling value-added services.

You should also recognize that the sales cycle to reach the top levels can be lengthy, probably measured in years. It depends on the point (level) at which you formally launch your alignment mission. While no one can give you an estimate of how long it takes to reach the business consultant or partner/ally levels, I can assure you that (1) it does take a long time and (2) you almost always have to take the linear path from spectator to the top. There are few shortcuts. On the other hand, if you have worked hard

> ## ⚑ RED FLAG continued
>
> and reached the preferred provider level, it may be relatively easy to move to the business consultant peak, and be done in short order.
>
> A lot of obstacles get in your way: time, constant changes in the account organization and marketplace, the fact that you may have to do as much internal selling within your own company as you will do externally with your customers.
>
> Finally, and most importantly, you will probably not get to the partner/ally level unless you have a defined corporate "partnership program" to help you. There will be exceptions, of course, but most of the salespeople and companies that get to the very top (and stay there) have a corporate mandate, resources, and sales tools that drive them toward this high-level business. They also have a proven record of success in helping other companies share and manage resources. In the process, they have carved out a concept, given it structure, wrapped it around their products, and invented a method to sell it.
>
> The good news is that without this type of support and program, you can still climb the mountain and achieve success at high levels. Because of these reasons, however, you need to move from one level to another, catching your breath at each before moving higher.

THE PATH TOWARD THE TOP

Because of the long sales cycle, there is no step-by-step model or pa for moving ahead in your alignment strategy. However, there are a nur ber of tactical steps that can be taken at each level, before you can a cend to the next plateau. The order will change from situation to situ tion, and some of the steps will be taken concurrently with others. most instances, all these tactical steps should be taken:

1. Define the alignment.
2. Sell the concept internally.
3. Develop superchampions.
4. Conduct research.
5. Design a proposal.
6. Test the proposal with the champions.

7. Sell the account's key players.

8. Manage the implementation.

In the pages that follow, each of these steps will be expanded on.

1.Define the Alignment

Before you can define where you want to go, you need to accurately assess where you are with a specific account. The AQ test will serve as a guideline and enable you to pinpoint clearly what level you are currently at: spectator, vendor, preferred provider, business consultant, partner/ally.

Next, you need to creatively (and realistically) determine if you can move ahead or maintain your position. This is a tough decision to make without a lot of account analysis (we'll talk more about that in the next chapter). However, let's assume you know your account, the people, the culture, and other driving forces pretty well. Consequently, you must determine if you want to stay at the current level (and continue to grow your business), or if the time and conditions are right to move to the next level. Sound easy? No way! Here's where the real creativity comes into play.

At this first step, you are challenged to define the alignment in one or two sentences. In other words, describe for yourself how the alignment will work in terms of (1) what it is and (2) how it will help you achieve the account's goals and bring value to the account. If you can't do this (and it will take lots of thought and creativity), don't go any further. This takes vision—the ability to look ahead and visualize how you can get to the next level. This definition is more than a goal. It's a strategic mission statement, describing *how* you can accomplish your goal. The statement should be realistic, based on your assessment, but it doesn't have to be specific at this point. It will serve as a final test to see if your strategy is doable and realistic. It will surface possibilities and help you move to the next step. No doubt it will change as you evolve the strategy and begin to implement it. Later in the process, goals can be added that state specific product sales, among other objectives.

Here are a few examples positioned at each level in which salespeople briefly describe how they will reach the next level:

Spectator level (currently): Get my foot in the door at XYZ Company by gaining access to Charley Gold (at vice president level) with the intention of showing him how our networking system can provide efficiency and improve communications.

Vendor level (currently): Become a preferred provider with ABC Company by "selling" them on our value-added, just-in-time delivery service for our pumps. This will eliminate inventory costs without investment.

Preferred provider level (currently): Gain access to top-level decision makers at Hardy Co. by doing ongoing quality/usage checks of our computer products, followed by semiannual business reviews.

Business consultant level (currently): Develop proposal for Large Corp. to manage its 85 in-store baking facilities, providing our people to supervise personnel and operations that are using our baking supplies.

It's easy to recognize the progression in scope from one level to another. However, this reinforces the facts: (1) It's difficult to jump more than one level at a time; and (2) lots of thought and creativity are required at this incipient stage in developing a strategic plan of action.

Are these strategic plans? No. Will the concept change? Yes. These defining statements are a jumping-off point to reasonably assess the possibility and then move on to another critical step. If you can't define your mission in one or two sentences, you should certainly continue to build the business, but you should remain at the same level for the time being. Perhaps, too, you simply have not put enough time, thought, and creativity into the process. Concerning the latter, we'll provide some tools and ideas for helping you scope out the account in the next and final chapter. These tools will provide the discipline to search for account opportunities that may then lead you to jump to the next level.

2. Sell the Concept Internally

If you're at the spectator level, you can probably skip this step. However, as you progress up the ladder, internal support is more critical at each step. This may be the toughest part of your sale! You must determine who needs to provide initial and ongoing support for undertakings of these magnitudes. Support includes both people and resources, and there's no sense in approaching a specific level unless you know you have the internal support you need.

How do you obtain this support? You generally need a proposal of sorts just as you would to sell any concept. Preferably it should be documented and you should present it to your own boss and other decision makers. Like most of the strategies we've covered in this book, you should spell out the values in terms of your organization's costs and potential gains (benefits). If you make this sale, then you can go back to your account strategy and move ahead. That's why it's critical to tie down the support commitment before you go ahead.

Here are some methods for accomplishing this. First, calculate your future company benefits. While sales management is interested in new accounts, greater account penetration, repeat business, and increased profit, everything is driven by sales improvement. One way to determine sales improvement (and present it to your boss and other key decision makers) is to forecast the future business to be gained. To do that, use the expected value (EV) formula with the individual account:

EV = Current sales + New business (Potential × Probability)

The current sales figure is your annual business, and that's easy to come by. New business is more difficult to get a handle on, but the formula will provide a simple and reliable forecasting method. First, you estimate the potential. In this case, potential is equal to all the business you are *not* getting plus a growth factor. Most of this potential currently resides with your competition. However, if the account is growing at a fast rate, you should add in a fudge factor to accommodate the growth. Finally, you need to provide an estimate of the probability of this happening. This is your success factor (and reality check) for achieving the level you are going for. The probability is a percentage—your gut feeling of how much of that extra business you can acquire with an intensive effort and a high degree of success.

Here's an example. An account manager does $1.5 million annually with an account, getting about 40 percent of the total business. This means there is another 60 percent potential business available, or $1 million. Based on some careful consideration, the account manager estimates this business will normally grow about 10 percent; in addition, the account manager estimates that she can take 15 percent of the total business via strategic planning and penetration. Therefore, the numbers in the formula look like this:

EV = $1,000,000 + ($1,650,000 × .15) = $1,247,500

When the account manager does internal selling, she can reasonably document about a 25 percent increase in business if the plan works. Not a bad gain!

A second reason for internal selling to gain support for a strategic plan is to document the projected cost of gaining this extra $250,000 worth of business. For example, you should look at costs like these and come up with realistic estimates:

- Sales and executive time (yours and others).
- Value-added services (these costs were covered in Chapter 4).
- Promotional merchandise/samples.
- Advertising and other direct funds.
- Other costs.

Let's suppose our account manager estimated she and others would have to allocate about 75 days out of a year to accomplish her goal. At $300 a day (her estimate), this time was worth $22,500. In addition, another $25,000 was needed to provide value-added services and $2,000 for out-of-pocket expenses. The total cost estimate, therefore, is about $50,000 to acquire approximately $250,000 worth of new business. Not a bad ROI! These numbers can then be used to sell internally and to use as a springboard for gaining support and commitment from key players. In other words, you need to be your own champion and make the internal sale before you try selling to the customer.

3.Develop Superchampions

In this scenario, where you are aligning with your customer, you are basically selling concepts, not product. The concept is the alignment and the champion(s) becomes much more important. Some general rules to be aware of:

- You will never sell an alignment concept without a champion.
- One champion will seldom get the job done.
- The higher the alignment level, the more champions you will need.
- Champions take a long time to develop, so start early in your strategic mission.
- The champions need to be thoroughly educated in your proposal before they sell to others.

- The champion, who is helping you sell a concept at the higher alignment levels (business consultant or partner/ally), must possess exceptional qualifications to get the job done.

Consider that you are selling concepts (intangibles) at these levels, rather than just product. So in addition to having need for a champion, you need someone that can grasp the concept and spread your cause with evangelical zeal. He or she must be totally sold on the concept first and then be willing to run through walls to achieve it. Commitment is not strong enough; the champion should be a zealot in search of the Holy Grail. The champion may be the most significant force in accomplishing your alignment at the top levels. Once sold on the concept, the right champion will drive it with persistence. Once the alignment is achieved, the champion will continue to make it work. The champion at these levels understands the challenges and risks but also sees the value for the organization and possibly for himself or herself. The champion will also provide you with feedback and will not hesitate to tell you if your concept has shortcomings. It takes work to identify and cultivate these super-champions, but it's the most expedient way to sell concepts and alignments at high levels.

4.Conduct Research

Good salespeople are constantly doing research, so this step or action is not a big deal. It's worth mentioning, however, that while you may be constantly improving your account learning curve, when it comes to alignment strategy there should be a higher-level focus on information required. In brief, you have to determine how agreeable the account is to the idea of alignment. Knowing how it measures success in alignments is also critical. Your research should surface some agreement on preliminary goals and measurements.

5.Develop a Proposal

The alignment strategy at the top levels mandates a written proposal, often backed by a formal group presentation. The key word for both events is *documentation*. You may use a short executive-briefing report style or a detailed proposal. In either case, it should follow a simple format—background, problems and opportunities, recommendations, budget, and so on. Most importantly, the document should explain

(1) how the alignment will operate; (2) the tangible values it will bring to the account (in financial terms where possible); (3) average success rates you experienced with other accounts; and (4) goals for this account. And if you give a group presentation, prepare visuals to document and sell your written proposal.

6.Test the Proposal with the Champions

You should get input from your champions at every stage or step. Be prepared to make changes or revisions, as needed, to accommodate their ideas and requests.

7.Sell the Account Players

Get buy-in up and down the line. The more the better! And be prepared to make revisions.

8.Manage the Implementation

At this point, you and your champions must determine what it will take to implement the alignment and what it will take to ensure success.

WHAT'S MISSING?

I hope you have a clue that something is missing from this alignment strategy, particularly when you get to the highest levels, business consultant and partner/ally. What's missing is a set of tools for making the alignment strategy work. What really makes this strategy happen are the *other strategies* we've discussed earlier: team selling, consultative selling, selling value-added services, sales negotiating, and access strategy. When it comes to the alignment strategy, You can "talk the walk," but you can't "walk the talk" without them. At some point in your alignment selling, when you get past the spectator level, you will need one or more of these strategies to make alignment work. Together, they provide the foundation, or the synergism, for moving up the mountain. Yes, they may be used piecemeal at different points or even used together. And while each of the five strategies can stand alone at the lower levels of alignment, most of them will be needed to provide consultation, to gain access, to add value, to negotiate issues, or to use a team strategy for selling the alignment.

The next chapter will deal with ways to merge these strategies so they flow together as one powerful piece of architecture. This is where the real creativity of strategizing occurs—in putting it all together. As Thomas Edison said:

"Anything that won't sell, I don't want to invent." He built on the base of others' creations, starting where the last person left off. Now that you've digested or reinforced a number of key sales strategies, you'll be challenged to build on this knowledge by inventing a major creative strategy (or strategies) that utilizes your experience in a simulated account.

8 CHAPTER

Putting It All Together

WHERE DO YOU GO FROM HERE?

If you have a good understanding of specific strategies gained from this book or your own experience, you may be wondering if this chapter is really necessary. Like the proverbial iceberg, you've only seen the tip—the small percent of the whole that is showing above the surface. What lurks beneath the water is the critical mass—the 90 percent that enables you to effectively put the strategies into play.

The challenge is not in execution of the strategy or strategies. It is (1) selecting the best strategic path or architecture for each account and (2) utilizing one or more strategies to get the job done. A strategic approach will not work every time; like sales skills, some will fail due to timing, competition, execution, or a wrong match with the situation or customer. However, there are fail-safe measures that a prudent salesperson can take to ensure a good match between the strategy and the situation. These measures won't guarantee success in every strategic situation, but they will fatten your batting average.

The answer lies in strategic account analysis to identify opportunities. Once identified, an architecture must be designed around the strategies to make them work together and to tie them into a cohesive plan. In earlier chapters, we've provided objectives for each strategy, which describe general situations where each strategy can be employed. However, when we introduce a specific account into the picture, the challenge is to identify an opportunity that matches the strategy. That's where the analysis comes in because it enables you to bare the soul of the account, to reinforce what you know, and to also "know what you don't know."

You're probably thinking: "Give me a break! I know my important accounts inside out." I would agree. The point is not the knowledge or information about the account that counts, it's how you analyze it. That is a significant challenge in becoming a sales strategist. It's a challenge because most salespeople don't like to do analytical tasks. In addition, in some account analyses, either heavy experience or a set of tools (or both) may be needed to do an effective job. Some of the tools will be provided here, but you'll have to provide the brain power. The good news is that you don't have to do analysis for *every* account, and, in cases in which account analysis is called for, you don't need to do it *often*. Once accomplished, an annual update is all that's needed to identify the changes and pinpoint new opportunities.

LET THE SEARCH BEGIN!

Account analysis, as discussed here, is simply searching for sales opportunities, then using strategic ploys to capitalize on them. How do you define an opportunity? An opportunity is a set of present or future circumstances requiring the account to use new solutions or approaches in which, with the right timing and resources, your organization could play a significant part. Some general examples of opportunities would include:

- A major change in the account organization.
- A specific problem that you could help solve.
- A trend that will impact the account's business.
- Matching your products/strategies with the account's goals.
- A competitive weakness.
- A new need or expanded one that your product can solve.
- New or different decision makers.
- A change in your product offering that requires different approaches.

These types of opportunities can surface in your normal selling activities, but you may learn of them after the fact. In addition, you might not see them as opportunities that strategies can solve, or you may fail to bring them into focus. In-depth analysis will both reinforce and focus. Analysis is a discipline that must be documented to highlight the trends, gaps, and problems that ultimately translate into opportunities. It's the best way to "get in the account's face," and it's the only effective method to identify opportunities and problems that you can match with your menu of strategies.

The key business opportunities in most organizations can be captured by using a series of templates or opportunity windows. Templates enable you to display and examine in depth the critical indicators of business success. The objective in each template is to find one or more opportunities. In other words, you focus on individual segments of the business to surface opportunities. Next, you try to connect the various opportunities, or select those that have highest priority, and build a strategic action plan to capitalize on them.

 C A S E   S T U D Y

SIMULATED ACCOUNT ANALYSIS

To set the stage for using templates that follow, we'll use a simulated situation (account) as a springboard for analysis. To make it more interesting, you will be challenged to analyze this situation (as you read it) using the information that a typical account manager might have. Your challenge will be to analyze without tools or templates the information that follows and to identify key opportunities and strategies for capitalizing on them. Afterward, we'll provide feedback on this simulated situation using sample templates to do the analysis.

*　　*　　*　　*

You are an account manager for the Hi-Tech Corp. (HIT), a major manufacturer of state-of-the-art computers and software. Your company is 20 years old; it has grown at a rate of 30 percent a year and, while not the largest in the industry, is now considered a major player. One reason for HIT's growth is its strategic approach to the marketplace. The major corporate strategy is wrapped around its integrated capability: HIT can provide a full line of computers (personal computers and servers), complete software, and total service/consulting backup. This integration gives you a competitive edge in an industry in which most of the hardware and software are produced by manufacturers of either equipment or software, but not both. There are few differences between your equipment and software and that of your competitors. In fact, the equipment (computers) being provided by most manufacturers resembles clones of all the others. In terms of software, there are occasional breakthroughs, but most, and to some degree all, have become commodities. There are two major operating systems driving the computers, the A system and the D system, and they are incompatible with one another. Your computers use the D system.

You manage 10 key accounts, including the Masters Corp. The Masters Corp. is a tool manufacturer with 16,000 people in the United States housed in 15 locations: headquarters, nine regional sales offices, and five manufacturing plants. Masters' annual sales are about $800 million, with profits in the 4 percent range (after taxes). Sales have plateaued in recent years with profits declining from 8 to 10 percent to the current level. As a public company, Masters is under heavy pressure to raise the profit level. It has recently undergone reengineering that has changed most of its processes. A direct result has been a downsizing of 20 percent of the workforce; last year it had 20,000 people, and it shed 4,000 people to get to its present size.

Masters has been a good account for you. Your business has grown at a healthy rate, and you have good relationships overall. Your overall sales volume for the last three years has been as follows:

Current year:	$940,000
Last year:	$822,000
Previous year:	$750,000

Your competitors for equipment in this account are Apricot (which uses the A operating system) and Clone Corp., a direct-mail competitor; Clone computers use the D system. The software purchases are made from many vendors, and the service is provided by a variety of local consultant and service organizations, along with yourself. Prices for all these items are reasonably competitive, since Masters has negotiated for similar levels of pricing for most computer-related products.

From information you've gathered, Apricot is the major computer provider; its sales over the same three-year period were as follows:

Current year:	$1,500,000
Last year:	$1,325,000
Previous year:	$1,280,000

Apricot sells and services its computers and software through its national dealer network. Apricot initially made its name in laptops but in recent years has moved heavily into the desktop personal computer arena. Because of graphics capabilities and user-friendly systems, most users are reticent to switch. In the instances in which you've done user conversions, you have provided extra training and technical "hand-holding."

Clone Corp.'s figures are as follows:

Current year:	$380,000
Last year:	$200,000
Previous year:	$110,000

Clone has a slight price advantage but does not market software and provides limited service: an 800 telephone help line and warranty service on new installations for 90 days.

You are unable to retrieve accurate figures on software purchases, but you received some estimates from an internal source that the total software cost of about $250,000 was allocated about 40 percent for Apricot, 30 percent for HIT (your computers), and 30 percent for all others.

Masters has three major goals for the next 12 months:

- To bring down operating expense.
- To target sales for profitability rather than volume.
- To improve its delivery and turnaround for all customers.

As part of developing a better sales cost ratio, Masters is hoping to automate its sales force (recently trimmed from 500 to 300 people) with laptop computers and special sales software, enabling salespeople to communicate/network with key departments. During the next 18 months, Masters will also address the more complex issue of improving customer service, reducing complaints, and maintaining market share. The strategy, you're told, will probably involve automating many other functions.

The decision makers and influencers that you're familiar with are:

- *Richard Krauss, Management Information Systems (MIS) manager.*
  Richard is your primary contact at Masters for software and equipment. He

is under a lot of pressure to produce results, and you wonder how long he'll last. He tends to be quietly demanding and highly analytical in his personal style. He asks pointed and detailed questions and will sit in unnerving silence until he feels they have been answered to his satisfaction. Richard has the expertise to discuss any of the technical issues that arise, but he is at least two levels removed from the key decision maker. He prefers the D system and, in most competitive situations, will specify HIT.

- *Mary Havermann, director of MIS.* Richard reports to Mary, who occasionally sits in on meetings. Compared to Richard, Mary is open and quite social. There are times when you have welcomed her presence, as when you and Richard have been at an impasse on one issue or another. Mary and Richard report in turn to Mark Helms, vice president of MIS. Richard tries to block you from meeting with Mary, unless he is involved.

- *Mark Helms, vice president of MIS.* Mark is, you theorize, a key decision maker most of the time. He is extremely focused, concise, and results oriented. On the few occasions when you have made presentations to Mark, you found him brusque, hard to read, and even a little arbitrary in making conclusions and decisions. According to your intelligence, Mark made all the decisions on laptop purchasing in a preliminary "request for proposal." Richard has told you that Mark doesn't like to deal with vendor salespeople.

- *The committee.* This year, major decisions regarding new equipment acquisitions will go to the Executive Policy Committee for final approval. Mark's recommendations to the committee will probably be the main source of influence on the committee. The committee consists of Mark Helms; Harry Evans, vice president of finance; Marjorie Hamilton, vice president of purchasing; and Ed Jones, vice president of sales.

You've also had dealings with purchasing, and other administrative functions, but the main focus is on the systems people in MIS.

As account manager, you have full responsibility for Masters, but when needed you can call Harry Gross or Tony Petrone, both technical directors in your region, specializing in hardware and software, respectively. In addition, your boss Chuck Adams, regional manager, is also available for backup support in both business issues and sales. If needed, you can also get some senior executive support for high-visibility projects.

Overall, you see Masters as a good account, but your biggest frustration is the upheaval and politics going on. Masters has been besieged by foreign competition and, being reluctant to change, is now faced with the backlash of reengineering and downsizing. Morale is not good, and many of the managers that you deal with are nervous about job retention. While Masters anticipates new products flowing in the next 6 to 12 months, it also recognizes that its sales force will have to carry the brunt of the load in an effort to reach a profitable sales volume.

Masters generally perceives HIT as a good supplier with excellent desktop hardware and software, but it has little knowledge or experience with your laptop line. While your laptops are very functional and fast, the line is relatively new. Priced at $4,000, they are very competitively priced and, feature for feature, rank with the better laptops on the market. On the other hand, Apricot has built its reputation as a manufacturer of fast, efficient laptops, with great graphics.

*　*　*　*

Based on this simulated situation, which provides many of the real-life scenarios and challenges you might encounter, what are the major opportunities that surface? What strategies would you employ (in addition to traditional selling) to capitalize on these opportunities? If you're up to this challenge, jot down your perceptions on a piece of paper; if desired, go back to the first page of the simulation and review the information in depth. In upcoming pages in this chapter, we'll share our analysis and take you through the process, using specific tools to make the job easier.

PICK UP THE TOOLS

Let's back up and go through a detailed analysis of this simulated account situation, using a set of templates that will help you focus on the main issues or indicators of an account's potential for penetration. There are no right or wrong answers, but your logic should tell you that the more you know about an account, the better you will be at scoping out the possibilities, the problems, and the opportunities. The trick is to organize the information into a format that can easily be analyzed. Once this is accomplished, you simply analyze the analysis, putting a spin on the information in order to formulate your strategy. This is not easy, but the salespeople who have great success with major accounts have been trained to do this or have the right tools to do it.

Let's consider another important point before we move on to the templates and actually use these tools. The templates provide a discipline. They force you to dig up information that you may not have filed away or retained in memory. In addition, the right tools are designed so they help you organize the information by "indicators," quite often triggering trends, gaps, changes, and opportunities! Finally, by organizing the data on paper (or computer software) you can visually make the connections and enhance your results.

The five templates that follow are generic—they fit most account situations. We've selected five critical areas to examine. In real life, depending on your own business, there might be other significant areas to research and analyze. Equally important, the information analyzed in each might be different and organized in other ways. The templates that follow are not discussed in order of priority.

Competition Template

Since competitors exist in every major account, their current positions and history need to be assessed for strengths, weaknesses, changes, and trends. In short, you need to periodically review what the competition is doing in specific accounts. For example:

- Is a new competitor lurking in the wings?
- Has a competitive weakness or problem surfaced?
- Is competitor X getting more aggressive with new products, selling effort, pricing, etc.?
- How is your share of the account's business changing?

Quite often these changes or trends will point to strategic moves that you can make. The template in Exhibit 8.1 provides one model for displaying this critical data so it can be analyzed for opportunities or problems.

This tool enables you to graphically compare the various competitive activity. In real life it might be done more effectively by breaking out a product-by-product comparison. But even in this shorthand-type of comparison, one or two "ahas" jump out. In particular, it's important to recognize (at an early stage) that Clone, while having a lesser share of the account's business, is growing at a dramatic rate of 85 percent! This number will surface only when you compare sales figures over time and delineate the trend. It's also useful to know that you are gaining on Apricot, even though you only have about half the current business that it has.

Other important information (or reinforcement) that comes from this analysis is the fact that you have some advantages over Apricot, but the main obstacle (for both companies) is that your operating systems are incompatible.

E X H I B I T   8 . 1

Strategic Match **Competition in This Account**			Problems/ Opportunities Scratch Pad
Our major competitors (direct and indirect) in this account	**Their strengths in this account**	**Their weaknesses in this account**	
1. Apricot Computer	Largest vendor	A operating system, not compatible with D system	
2. Clone Corp.	Lower price	Limited service	
3.			
Us	**Our strengths**	**Our weaknesses**	
(HIT)	Full service, good relationships	Not as well known as Apricot, not compatible	

Sales/Product Penetration						Problems/ Opportunities Scratch Pad
Your product	Sales analysis			Account share	Market share	Growth rate in account:
Competition	Previous year	Last year	Current year	(%)	(%)	
1. Hit	$ 750,000	$ 822,000	$ 940,000	33	6	12%
2. Apricot	$1,280,000	$1,325,000	$1,500,000	53	12	8%
3. Clone	$ 110,000	$ 200,000	$ 380,000	14	4	85%!!
						Watch out for Clone!

What are the possible opportunities that might surface from this analysis?

1. Watch your back! Clone is moving in fast, obviously because of a slight price edge. You can convert this to an opportunity by capitalizing on Clone's inability to provide service.

2. The incompatibility between Apricot and your operating systems will ultimately be a problem for Masters. At some point, Masters will be forced to standardize, so you'd better move quickly on this opportunity.

Relationship Management Template

Relationship, as you know, is largely a function of selling skills (as opposed to strategy), and it's something you learn by "living in the account" on a daily basis. However, relationships become the springboard for strategy execution, and unless you have developed a strong set of relationship building blocks, you will not have a potential strategic match. In this instance, however, the match seems good, and you may use these relationships as a conduit for implementing your strategic plan. In Exhibit 8.2, you must ask yourself some penetrating questions and provide realistic answers. The template provides a discipline for thinking through and analyzing critical account relationship indicators. Would you routinely ask yourself *all* of these questions without a tool to trigger them? As the current Hertz commercial goes: "Not exactly!" I won't go through each question in detail, but let's focus on the ones that surface or buttress business opportunities.

Questions 1 to 5 reinforce the fact that there is a match. Hence, they underline the point that relationships are good, in general, and that you have the ability to meet future needs. Everything is on "go" so far. Question 5, in particular, is another reality check: You are currently stuck at the vendor level and it's time to align yourself as a preferred provider (or even make the jump to business consultant).

Question 7 indicates that your future efforts should focus on measurable results (this is essential at the business consultant and partner/ally levels). Your answer to Question 8 is a cue that you need to start building relationships at higher levels. Question 10 is a question you must ask yourself and come up with a positive answer. Particularly in this situation, where products are commodity-like, you will need to

Strategic Match *Relationship Management*	Problems/ Opportunities Scratch Pad
Overall, how does this account view us in terms of . . .	
1. Our position in the industry? *Major player, but not #1*	
2. Our understanding of their business? *Good*	
3. Our *willingness* to meet their needs? *Excellent*	
4. Our *ability* to meet their needs? *OK*	

5.   Our current business relationship with them? (Check one)
 	
          X Vendor
          ___ Preferred provider
          ___ Business consultant
          ___ Partner/ally
	*Now is time to
	move to next level.*

6. Our reputation and image? *Solid*	
7. The results we have achieved for them? *Not measurable so far*	
8. Me personally? *Satisfactory relationships at middle levels*	*I need to build relationships at top.*
9. Others from our organization who interface with them? *Backup people get good marks*	
10. Our ability to provide value-added resources? *Fair; overall service = strong*	*This could give us an edge.*

differentiate yourself somehow from both Apricot and Clone. Value-added services may be your opportunity to distinguish yourself from the competition.

In this case, all the other questions reinforce the fact that your relationship-management indicators are in good shape for the match. Through analysis, the main opportunities that surface here are: (1) It's time to raise your sights and align yourself at a higher level, and (2) you better start thinking about value-added services as a vehicle for account penetration.

Needs-Identifier Template

This tool, or one like it, helps you focus on, and prioritize, account business needs. Exhibit 8.3 lists a global set of business needs and then requires that the user (account manager) do the following: (1) identify the needs and (2) match his or her company's ability to meet those needs.

Why is this indicator necessary (and helpful)? Typically, when you sell piecemeal (product selling), you sell to product needs and applications. Not so with strategies, as implied a number of times in this book. With strategies, you must focus on business needs and those with high priority, hence the "needs-identifier" template.

This template helps identify the overall corporate priorities and direction. First, it pinpoints Masters' priorities, some of which overlap and some of which individual executives may not even be aware. For example, it's very obvious Masters needs profits, but you can't contribute to that very much unless you can help it generate sales and improve efficiency (savings in overhead). Therefore, here are two interacting opportunities that match up with the company's needs and, in the process, make strategic selling a powerful and timely fit:

1. The key opportunity is equipping the sales force with laptops, since it will ostensibly improve sales and communication with headquarters. While this is a hot goal for you that could double your sales in the short term, it's much more important in the long term. Whoever wins this sale, because of the different operating systems, will "own" this account.

2. A supporting opportunity is that the vendor will need to provide uniform service for the field locations where the laptops are being used. While Apricot may have the edge in laptop hardware, you have the edge in the service area.

Both of these hot buttons will help you drive your strategy and reinforce the fact that you have to give this laptop opportunity your very best strategic shot.

Decision-Making Template

The decision-making template, as you'll notice in Exhibit 8.4, is a shortcut to mapping your strategy to gain account access.

In brief, it triggers information relating to four questions. Who makes purchase decisions? Who makes business (strategic) decisions? What is your access to each? What is the basic decision process for a major commitment?

E X H I B I T   8 . 3

Strategic Match

Needs Identifier

Prioritize the account's top 4 business needs by placing the numbers 1 to 4 in the boxes next to the appropriate needs. (1 = most important) Then, place a check next to those top 4 account needs you are best suited to meet.

Account's Needs	Priority Level (1–4)	Our Ability to Meet	Problems/ Opportunities Scratch Pad
Profit	1	√	*(Indirectly)*
Expansion			
Sales	2	√	*Can we get laptop sales contract?*
Service		√	
New products			
New markets			*They don't see service as an important need.*
Market share			
Cost savings			
Labor savings			
Productivity			
Systems	4	√	
Quality			
Efficiency	3	√	
Image			
Relationship			
Other: ————			
Other: ————			

How well do *they* think we meet their top 4 needs?

Good match

How well *could* we meet their top needs? What would it take?

1. *Need laptop business from sales*
2. *Standardize on one system*

E X H I B I T 8 . 4

Strategic Match		Problems/ Opportunities Scratch Pad
Decision Making		
Who are the key players in the account (including consultants, if applicable) who . . .		
Make purchase decisions?		
Richard Krauss, MIS manager	(1)	
Implement and support purchase decisions?		
Mary Havermann, director of MIS	(2)	
Bill Balinski, purchasing agent	(1)	
Make strategic business decisions?		
Mark Helms, vp of MIS	(3)	I must get to higher-level people!
Harry Evans, vp of finance	(3)	
Ed Jones, vp of sales	(3)	
Implement and support strategic business decisions?		
All of the people on the committee		
Make decisions? ☐ Decision maker ☐ Committee ☑ Consensus ☐ Undefined/vague ☐		
Next to each name above, indicate how accessible they are to you. (1 = very, 2 = moderately, 3 = not very)		

If you use this template in examining the Masters account situation, it underlines the following general strategic opportunities:

1. Access at higher levels is a *must*!

2. It's critical to build a strategy for accessing the committee. More specifically, it indicates a need to get to Mark Helms, vice president of MIS; Harry Evans, vice president of finance (remember *profit* need); and Ed Jones, vice president of sales.

The bottom line for this template is that the access strategy is badly needed if you are going to capitalize on these potential opportunities.

Measures of Success Template

The final tool, which might be applicable in assessing the match between your capabilities and the account's needs, primarily looks at measures. If a major account is committed to looking at specific, measurable results, you'd better be in a position to provide them. This can be done in the selling process (to justify the sale), and afterward a mechanism can also be set up to track results and improvements. In either case, you should acquire a better understanding of the account's expectations for measurement. The sample template in Exhibit 8.5 provides a model for our simulated account.

This template reinforces the fact that Masters is in a tough growth-and-profit situation. Its key decision makers will look long and hard at every decision, due to the need to turn the business around; there will be no risk takers in this downsized environment. Consequently, decision makers will challenge presentations from vendors who claim past successes elsewhere, and they will expect a forecast of future results. They will certainly not spend money unless they can make money as a result. These findings/conclusions indicate a potential need for strategies that employ measurements, return on investment data, and documented proof, particularly in bottom line dollars supported with success stories elsewhere.

HOW DO YOUR OPPORTUNITIES/STRATEGIES COMPARE?

Earlier in this chapter, you were challenged to read through a hypothetical account situation and try to identify key opportunities and strategies. There are no right or wrong answers, of course. If you analyzed this account situation without templates, you should be comparing the processes. Which was easier? Which method provided more conclusions, facts, opportunities, and strategies?

To summarize, here are the major opportunities that have surfaced, based on the information generated from the five templates. Some of the opportunities have been combined, and next to each is indicated a potential strategy that can be employed to capitalize on the opportunity. The opportunities, presented in order of priority, are:

E X H I B I T   8 . 5

Strategic Match			Problems/ Opportunities Scratch Pad
Account's Measures of Success Check off how the account measures success and what we can measure.			
	How Account Measures Success	**What Can We Help Them Measure?**	
Sales	√	√	*How can we provide measures?*
Profits	√	*indirectly*	
Market share?	?		
Productivity	√	√	*We need to sell value and services.*
Customer satisfaction			
Other:			
Other:			

Current Growth Mode		Problems/ Opportunities Scratch Pad
Account growth: —— High —— Moderate —√— Low —— Flat —— Negative	Our growth in the account: —√— High —— Moderate —— Low —— Flat —— Negative	

Values/Image/Culture		Problems/ Opportunities Scratch Pad
Describe the account's values, image, and culture: • *Need profit and growth* • *People nervous due to downsizing, changes*	Our values, image, and culture: *Quality service products and services at fair prices*	*Decision makers will not take risks.*

Major Opportunities	Strategies Needed
1. Sell laptops to sales force on basis of *value, service, result measurements*	Access, team selling, consultative selling
2. Replace Apricot system, selling need for efficiency (compatible systems)	Value-added selling, alignment strategy

Strategic Priority 1

The first priority—selling laptops to the sales force—is obvious. No red-blooded salesperson would walk away from it. However, the development of the strategy and the strategic tools you might employ require more thought and analysis. One solution is to use three strategies in concert to make the ultimate sale. The access strategy is critical to get you in front of the high-level decision makers and the committee. In the process, you may uncover other decision makers and influencers. Team selling strategy is required also, possibly bringing experts (technical and financial, for example) into play on team calls and a group presentation to the committee.

However, the main problem or challenge here is selling against Apricot's line of laptops. The challenge for the account manager in this case (aside from reaching higher levels and using team resources) will be to differentiate the offering. This can't be done with the hardware, but it can be done successfully with value-added benefits and actual service. However, to develop your "case" for this, you could employ consultative selling. You can focus on two of the interacting business needs surfaced in our analysis (service and value) and use them to differentiate yourself. HIT has, and Apricot may not have, the capability to service laptops in many remote locations on a consistent basis because of its dealer network. This is a potential problem in search of a solution. Masters may not be aware of the potential problem and you can certainly bring it to the decision makers' attention. Related to that is the service quality itself, which may include recommending appropriate software and being able to provide training to the sales force.

Assuming this is a valid approach, Consultative selling strategy can provide data and documentation that will define the potential problem in advance and put a value on the parameters. What's required, as part of the strategy, is field research to compare service points and possibly response times. Buy-in to this concept will be required from the vice president of sales so that you can invest some time interviewing sales managers and contacting salespeople to define and measure their service needs and assess their software requirements. MIS will certainly help. You can study the implications of downtime (waiting for service) and its impact on sales force effectiveness. Ultimately, you need to understand and document these issues so you are armed with data when you present. If this sounds complicated, it's what's required to differentiate yourself in this situation. There are many routes to take, of course, but this illustrates the creativity and depth of planning required to pursue a major piece of business. The initial laptop sale for the Masters sales force is in excess of $1.2 million, and software/service costs would enlarge that figure.

This is not an easy sale, but there's little chance it would be made without a strategic plan, since Apricot has some advantages, and other competitors might be asked to bid. Strategic selling is the only way to position yourself for a win of this magnitude. In this situation, a win will also provide you with the momentum to move to the second opportunity.

Strategic Priority 2

Most experts would agree that a win in the first situation is needed to move ahead with the second strategic priority. This differs from the first opportunity in that this strategic approach requires a much longer time frame, and to initiate it you probably need to move up the alignment ladder to preferred provider. You are now a preferred provider, assuming you won the laptop contract. To move to the next level, you will become a business consultant. The challenge is to make Masters Corp. more efficient, more productive, and more profitable by helping to handle its management information systems (computers, software, and service). The lead-in for this is the displacement of Apricot over time. In this simulated situation, there's a strong need for all computers to communicate with each other. Since you are the preferred provider, it may be time to initiate your strategy and design a plan to gradually replace the competition.

Basically, you need to delve in depth into the customer's computer operations—helping them run more efficiently and profitably. The critical wedge is the linkage between all computers (your area of expertise), so you need to allocate some resources (value-added) to help accomplish this. In real life, because of the complexity of this approach and the knowledge you might possess, you could take many routes to move up to a business consultant. This strategy will take time, spanning a year or more, and you will use many interwoven strategies along the way. For example, at some point you may have to initiate a negotiation strategy, even employ team selling. They all fit together and ultimately become one master strategy.

If you haven't utilized in-depth strategic approaches like this, you can see the complexity and the creativity that's involved. These are real challenges for the sales strategist, but certainly worth the time and effort for high-potential accounts. You may be wondering how often this analysis should be done. In-depth analysis on an annual basis will be adequate for most major accounts. However, you need updates to keep up with changes and progress as your penetration moves forward. We've provided you with much of the information in our simulated Masters account; in real life you will have much of this information stored in your database and account records, but you will no doubt have to do a "due-diligence" search to find the real valuable information on decision makers, competition, and so on. However, there's another need and yet another challenge. You're almost there, but not quite.

STAYING ON TRACK

Strategic selling, as implied throughout, is primarily a cognitive ability—the ability to think. While selling skills are also critical, it's the thought process that holds the process together. Until now, you've employed other cognitive abilities: analysis and strategy selection. A third "thinking" skill is planning—putting together a dynamite scheme that will get you where you want to go. So far, the process is this: You've analyzed a situation to identify opportunities, then selected strategies that might be employed individually (or together) to achieve your sales goals. What's missing is a concrete plan of action.

No long-term strategy can be successfully implemented without a written action plan. There are many reasons this is critical. First, a strategy is a route with many steps (tactics) along the way. Would you drive from Los Angeles to New York without carefully mapping the way? Of course not. You need to plan your strategy route in similar fashion, with sufficient detail to get you moving in the right direction. Unlike traveling cross-country, your strategy map will be filled with detours, blockades, and a pothole or two. Driving a route and driving a strategy are similar in some ways, but different in others. The dilemma you face along the strategic path is the dynamics of the account, the fact that every tactic will not work, and that you are aiming at a moving target. But that's just another reason you need to carefully design the architecture for your plan. You dodge the detours and problems by (1) constantly adjusting your plan on a short-term basis and (2) building in contingencies, where possible.

It's essential to have a plan and particularly important to document it in written format so it serves as a communication tool. It enables you to visualize the major steps, to communicate to team members, and to determine needed resources. Most importantly, it's a communication tool for yourself, geared to trigger the adjustments needed if you go off track and to provide you with the discipline to follow the path.

The paradox in strategic planning is that while your "sale" may be a year or two away, you can't plan that far in advance. You need the vision (and the strategy) in advance to see the entire route, but because of the obstacles and dynamics, you can do your in-depth planning only on a short-term basis. This means you really need this plan. The strategic plan keeps the big picture, the long haul, in focus. But you should supplement it with a series of short-term plans. Quarterly planning works best for most strategic salespeople and companies, but monthly or even semiannual action plans will also work. In any case, it's imperative to see this short-term plan as part of your overall long-term strategic game plan; if not, you might revert to piecemeal tactics and sales calls that have little fit with your overall strategic game plan.

THE STRATEGIC ACTION PLAN

The hands-on tool in strategic planning is the action plan. That's where the implementation occurs. That's where you get the payback for your planning and strategizing efforts. A strategic action plan is nothing more than a short-range tactical map of what you plan to do, when, how, and with whom. It's an action plan complete with timetables and designated resources you intend to employ. It should be done in sequential steps, planning for activities such as sales calls, research, meetings, formal presentations, and internal sessions with your own company personnel.

Because of the volatile (and often unpredictable) nature of face-to-face sales, competitive reactions, the challenge of getting to decision makers, overcoming obstacles, and unforeseen changes, the implementation of action planning must be short term to ensure flexibility and success! Long-range goals and strategies dictate the path you follow to get from one point to another; the action plan allows you to adjust your short-term tactics and plans to keep on track and ultimately achieve your long-range results. Consequently, the strategic action plan should be revamped frequently, to allow you to shift tactics as necessary. In some industries, your planning will follow the sales or promotional cycle (e.g., every six weeks); in others, it can be done as needed.

The strategic action plan should reflect both your long-range goals and strategies for achieving them, along with any results/adjustments that have been triggered by your previous action plan.

In using a strategic action plan, like the one in Exhibit 8.6 for the Masters account, keep these important guidelines in mind:

1. Establish objectives for the account, considering the period or overall timetable for the plan. Objectives are essentially short-term goals, or subgoals, and like a long-range goal they must be specific, customer oriented, and ambitious, but attainable.

2. Determine your steps or tactics, which are the individual "moves" for achieving your objectives, then organize them in order of implementation. Recognize that the steps or tactics typically involve more than just sales calls, although sales calls are obviously very important. For example, tactics may involve meetings with other members of your sales team or your boss, customer entertainment, research at account operating outlets, or they may even require nonselling calls to collect data, evaluate progress, probe for information, and implement a test.

3. Establish target dates for accomplishing each major step. This is not meant to place self-imposed restrictions on your efforts, but rather to generate both commitment and results. While flexibility is always important in selling, target dates will enable you to track and maintain your focus.

4. Anticipate obstacles for each major step or tactic. Even the best plans contain pitfalls and traps, so if you can anticipate objections, resistance, or blockage at different levels, you can develop methods to overcome them.

5. Plan to use all your resources. Your resources may involve members of your sales team, specialists, value-added services, other customers or decision makers (who can lend support), or sales tools such as data, multimedia presentations, or samples.

EXHIBIT 8.6 Strategic Action Plan

Account Name _Masters Corp._

Goal _Laptop order for salesforce ($1-2 million +)_   Date _12/29_

Strategy _Gain access, Team Selling, Consultative Selling_

For period ending _First quarter (3/31)_   Prepared by _J. R., account mgr., HIT_

Objectives: _Gain access to top level fast, differentiate ourselves from Apricot by documenting service values (savings)_

Steps/Tactics	Target Dates	Obstacles/ Methods to Handle	Resources Needed	Contingency Plan
Sales call on Ed Jones, vp of sales	1/10	May get bounced to director of sales, Tony White		See director of sales and get him to set up Jones call
Set up team and do briefing on account	1/12		Need tech plus regional vp support	
Meet with Richard and Mary/ present concept plan	1/20	Get them to set appointment with Mark Helms		Do top-to-top call with HIT MIS support vp
Send e-mail to our account managers	2/2		Need help at local levels (account managers)	
Get OK from Jones or White to do laptop-needs analysis	2/15	Pick sample of 30 (10%) geographic market of locales	Administrative coordination	
Chuck Adams to call Harry Evans	3/1		Financial projections	
Do focus group with sales department	3/16	Need their input!	Bring Harry Gross; do over lunch	Make individual calls
Team briefing in assigning sales calls	3/21		Set up telephone conference	

6. Develop contingencies. You can design contingencies while you put your plan together, or you may use the contingency plan column to make notes on necessary adjustments in your tactics as you take each step. It's essential to recognize that some ploys and tactics will fail, while others will succeed. When you can anticipate and protect your strategy against failure, you're way ahead; that's where contingency planning comes in.

Strategic planning is a continuous process, involving intensive analyses of the high-potential account to discover new opportunities and developing long-range goals and strategies for achieving them. To be effective, account analysis should be done at least once a year with frequent updates and adjustments. The direct output of the analysis should be a series of evolving, short-range strategic action plans, done one at a time. Each action plan should dovetail with the previous one, interweaving with your long-range goals and strategies for the account.

If you take a few minutes to look at some of the details in Exhibit 8.6, you'll see that our fictional account manager is supporting the strategy with specific tactics and even overlapping some of the strategies (via tactics). This action plan is the initial one for Masters and demonstrates the early steps and tactics for executing the mission.

THE BOTTOM LINE

You may be thinking that being a sales strategist requires a lot of work. However, it's significantly less than what's demanded for tactical selling. Regardless, in today's marketplace, you don't have a choice. In complex sales situations (Aren't they all?), you need an edge over the competition. Products alone won't do it, nor will great selling skills by themselves. Good sales tools will help, and a knowledge of sales strategy is very important, but the most critical element is *you,* the sales strategist. If you haven't changed with the times, you need to. One of the most important and demanding changes you will have to make, if you haven't already started, is to *think* and *act* strategically. If this book hasn't convinced you, then I've failed to communicate the concept.

While this book has covered specific strategies and provided models or guidelines for implementing them, the bottom line is that strategies are creative, flexible, and unlimited—and each has to be customized to a specific situation. Sitting on the bottom line is the sales strategist who must put the strategy into play and make it work.

I'd be remiss if I didn't provide a job description for today's sales strategist, recognizing that even these specifications will change as we move into the 21st century. Below are specific competencies that today's sales strategist needs. You may possess many of these competencies. We hope you will be motivated to grow to a point where you can be a master of them all.

THE SALES STRATEGIST JOB DESCRIPTION

Important *sales* competencies:

- Selling/communication skills.
- Product/account knowledge.
- Planning and organizational skills.
- Relationship-building skills.
- Work ethic.
- Competitive spirit.

Important *strategic* competencies:

- Creativity.
- Analytical skills.
- Problem-solving ability.
- Knowledge of sales strategies.
- In-depth knowledge of business operations.
- Vision and discipline to execute a strategic plan.

How do you measure up to these important competencies? We hope there's a close match, but if not, you will certainly recognize the gaps and aim to fully develop your strategic skills, competencies, and abilities. Your challenge is to change with the times and the marketplace, recognizing that strategic selling is a requirement for success. So go for it! The risks are minimal, and the rewards are great!

INDEX

A

Access strategy
  case studies utilizing, 9
  and the importance of being aware of responses, 109
  introduction to the, 99-100
  model for the, *see* Access strategy model
  tactics of the, *see* Access strategy model
Access strategy model
  overview of the, 100-101
  tactic(s) of the
    analyze the decision maze as a, 103-111
    deal with four levels of commitment as a, 115-117
    gain access as a, 112-115
    identify key players as a, 101-102
Account analysis
  analyzing the simulated, 145-153
  a case study of simulated, 141-145
  introduction to, 139-140
  summarizing the opportunities from the, 153-157
  what, is, 140-141
Action plan
  developing an, 79-80, 88-90
  initiating the team, 23-24
  staying on track with the, 157-158
  the strategic, 158-161
Ad hoc sales team, 17, 20
Alignment quotient (AQ), 123
Alignment quotient indicator, 123-125
Alignment strategy
  case studies utilizing the, 127-130
  defining, 120
  determining what makes the, work, 137-138
  examples of, 126-127
  five levels of alignment in the, 120-123

Alignment strategy—*Cont.*
  overview of, 119
  pitfalls of the, 130-131
  tactical steps to take in the, 131-137
  using the alignment quotient indicator in the, 123-125
Alliances, 3, 4
Apparent withdrawal tactic, 95-96
Attitude questions, 44-45

B

Business consultant, 121, 127, 133
Buyers, 3

C

Champion, 106, 115, 137
  super-, 135-136
Coaching, 27
Coach tactic, 112-113
Commitment
  dealing with the four levels of, 115-117
  four degrees of, 106-107
Competition, assessing the, 84, 86
Competition template, 146, 148
Computer data systems, 126
Consensus questions three types of, 29
Consequence questions, 45
Consultant, 35
  business, 121, 127, 133
  defining the term, 33
Consultative salesperson, 40
  methods and tools available to the, 48-49

ABOUT THE AUTHOR

Warren Kurzrock has spent his entire business career successfully selling—steel, business systems, services, products, and ideas. Now CEO of New York-based Porter Henry & Co., Inc., a leading sales force training and consulting firm, he still spends significant time in the field consulting with Fortune 500 clients and training their sales forces to sell more effectively.

Warren and his Porter Henry staff have pioneered, enhanced, and validated the strategies shared in this how-to book. The strategies are real-world, workable, and state of the art. Every salesperson and sales executive will gain new strategic techniques, tools, and ideas that have "Monday morning applicability." They will also learn why strategic selling is a must for the 1990s as we move into the 21st century.

A member of many professional sales and marketing organizations, Warren is a frequent speaker at meetings and conventions. He has published articles on selling and sales strategy in *Sales and Marketing* Magazine, the *American Society for Training and Development Journal,* and *Training* Magazine. Warren holds a BA degree from Duke University and an MBA from NYU Graduate School of Business.

Other books of interest to you from Irwin Professional Publishing . . .

THE ALLIGATOR TRAP

How to Sell Without Being Turned into a Pair of Shoes

Edward R. Del Gaizo, David J. Erdman, and Kevin Corcoran

Authored by president and executive staff of sales and service training leader, Learning International, *The Alligator Trap* is written for all salespeople—from the rookie to the seasoned veteran. Based on solid research and first-hand experience, it is smartly organized into four pratical, simple-to-read sections: Establishing the customer relationship; Building basic skills; Identifying buying attitudes; Partnering for the long-term.

0-7863-0856-7

SOCRATIC SELLING

How to Ask the Questions that Get the Sale

Kevin R. Daley with Emmett Wolfe

Shows salespeople how to build a relationship with the customer and close the sales more surely. The Socratic approach respects the power of the customer. The customer has the need, the power, and the decision-making authority. This book shows the reader how to access that power, to cooperate with it, and to induce it to flow toward the salesperson.

0-7863-0455-3

HIGH PERFORMANCE SALES ORGANIZATIONS

Creating Competitive Advantage in the Global Marketplace

Kevin J. Corcoran, Laura K. Petersen, Daniel B. Baitch, and Mark TerHarr

Filled with solid strategies, best practices, and provocative points of view that every organization can apply immediately. Companies will be able to compete more successfully by focusing on the new expectations of today's more demanding customers, developing a strategy to differentiate personal sales organization from today's more determined competitors, using best practices to ensure the successful execution of your sales strategy, and creating market-focused sales and service operations.

0-7863-0352-2

MANAGE GLOBALLY, SELL LOCALLY

The Art of Strategic Account Management

A. Lee Blackstone

Addresses the factors that make managing the account relationship different from territory management, offers tools to help the account manager measure success of position within the account. Ideally suited for organizations with an account-focused sales force selling complex products to global accounts, this unique guide outlines how a team approach can be used to successfully sell at all levels of the customer's organization.

0-7863-0330-1